GO INTO THE HOUSE

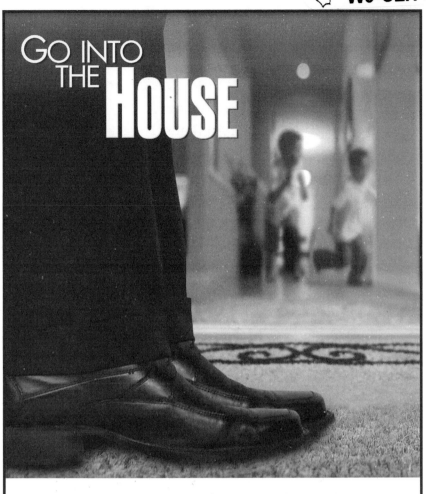

RODNEY A. WINTERS

FOGHORN
PUBLISHERS
"Of Making Many Books There Is No End..."

Go Into the House

ISBN-10: 1-934466-15-8
ISBN-13: 978-1-934466-15-5
Printed in the United States of America
©2009 by Rodney A. Winters. All Rights Reserved.

Foghorn Publishers
P.O. Box 8286
Manchester, CT 06040-0286
860-216-5622
foghornpublisher@aol.com
www.foghornpublisher.com

Acknowledgments

I'd like to gratefully acknowledge the continued support of the following people:

My Dad & Mom—Mrs. Kenneth C. Winters, Sr.—for your continued love and support.

Kara & Avery—the most loving kids a parent could ask for.

Randy Key—a true friend and brother.

Dr. Willis Lonzer III—for your long-term friendship.

André Patton—for being there during the dark, rough times.

Pastor William T. Hunt—my shepherd and partner in ministry.

Dr. Kevin R. Dudley—for your mentorship in ministry.

Pastor Bill Mitchell—for your friendship, counsel and encouragement.

Melissa Powell—for motivating me and giving your valued observations.

Dr. Wanda Davis-Turner—for your advice, encouragement, and introductions.

Dr. Aaron D. Lewis, JoAnna Laiscell-Brown and the fine staff at Foghorn Publishers.

Table of Contents

Introduction

For years I believed that I did not have a testimony for the Lord. I would hear people testify about how God had delivered them from drugs, alcohol, or a life of sexual promiscuity. I would also hear about how God healed others from a terminal disease like cancer, or a debilitating condition such as arthritis. I didn't have that type of experience. I grew up in a Christian home. My family went to church every Sunday and was active in our congregation. My parents were leaders in the church. I got saved around the age of five, so I was not exposed to a lot of negative influences. I didn't commit the major sins that people always talked about. I didn't smoke, drink or use drugs. I was far from perfect, but I generally lived a good life, by the power of the Holy Spirit. Other Christians would tell me I lived a sheltered life, and hadn't been through anything.

Even as a child I realized I was sheltered to an extent, and tried to make myself tougher. Part of my issue was my small size. I was very skinny, and didn't want to be perceived as a weakling. I would try to see how much physical pain I could endure. I would hold my arms out until they burned from the lack of oxygen. I would see how long and how hard I could pinch myself before I couldn't bear it anymore. When I got whippings from my parents (which was pretty often), I would force myself not to cry. This often meant a longer and harder whipping. On the playground I learned how to talk tough, even though I did not have the physical stature to back it up. Fortunately, I didn't have to attempt to back up my words very often. Until very recently, I had never been able to swallow pills, so when I have a headache, or any other kind of pain, I just stuck it out. I have developed a high tolerance for pain.

Some years ago, the Lord showed me that I really did have a testimony. It was a testimony of His keeping power. He kept me from the things that others had been delivered from. I never experienced waking up with a hangover, or waking up not knowing the person in bed with me. I don't know what it feels like to be high. I learned that I had no less of a testimony because I had not done things that others had done. This was a powerful revelation to me. God's keeping power is as great as His deliverance power. Then it seemed that not long after discovering I had a positive testimony, I lost it. It took years to build a reputation, and only a moment to lose it. I could no longer say I had been kept from certain things. I was a man that people once looked up to; now people were looking down on me.

My aim with this book is to share my testimony in hopes of encouraging other men on their Christian journey, especially as it relates to a difficult or failed marriage. I believe there is a purpose for the experiences I have undergone. There is some-one else who can benefit from my pain. I have not heard many men share the kinds of experiences I have encountered, but I know I am not alone. Men who have gone through similar circumstances as mine often do not have other men they share their struggles with. These are not easy experiences to share. I trust that this book will bring a fresh perspective on some issues that many men face. I am able to comfort others with the comfort with which I have been comforted. Even before completing this writing, I have been able to help others who were going through marital difficulty, through my personal experiences.

Now, more than ever, I have a burden for married couples. Marriages are under attack, as well as the institution of marriage itself. I wish I could teach other couples in a church classroom setting. Unfortunately, those opportunities are nonexistent in church settings I have seen. No divorced person is deemed qualified to teach on marriage. Marriage classes are only taught by married people. The thinking seems to be, how can a person who could not remain married teach someone else about the commitment required in marriage? I would agree that it would be difficult for someone who has never been married to teach on the subject, but one who has experienced it can bring some insight to those who are currently united in matrimony, or contemplating doing so.

Sometimes we can learn from the mistakes of others, as well as the positive experiences. For example, an adult can teach a teenager about surviving the teenage years, even though he or she is no longer a teenager. The fact that he or she was once a teenager still brings validity to his or her perspective. A nine-year old could not teach on being a teenager, but certainly an adult could. In the same way, a former alcoholic can counsel a person who is struggling with this addiction.

I have seen cases in which the married couples teaching the marriage class really do not have a good relationship with one another. The assumption seemed to be that just because they had been married for a number of years, they were qualified to teach the class. That is not always the case.

Similarly, most marriage books are written by people who have good and long-lasting marriages. I have personally benefited from these authors. I believe through years of counseling couples with troubled marriages and divine insight from the Word of God, these men and women are fully qualified to speak on the subject. With this book, I bring the perspective of someone who has been through the dark valley of a difficult marriage and subsequent divorce, and has come through on the other side. I'm a living witness that there is hope.

Women as well can gain insight from this book... Pain is not gender-specific. Anyone who has gone through a difficult circumstance in life can relate at some level. There may be a woman reading this book who has struggled with similar issues. I pray that she will see the impact of these issues on herself and others, and seek God's help to overcome.

I have run into so many people who tell me about the place in which they find themselves in life, and how things have not turned out they way they expected. For the most part it has not been through any fault of their own. They have done the right thing, yet the actions of others have caused them to find themselves in a difficult situation. Abuse, poverty, divorce, abandonment have left their toll on countless lives. There are those of you reading this now who are suffering through an injustice. Maybe no one else even knows about it. You may be saying to yourself, "what's the use?" "It doesn't pay to do right." But if you can just make your way into the house, you will find the shelter, comfort, nourishment, rest, and even celebration that you're looking for in the presence of our loving heavenly Father.

As a child, I often heard the phrase, "Go in the house." Sometimes it was in a negative context. It may have meant that I had gotten into trouble while playing outside, and my punishment was to go inside. There was usually a belt waiting on me when I got there. Sometimes it just meant that play time was over, or it had started to rain. There were also occasions when this phrase was a positive command. There was something in the house that I needed at the time. Maybe it was a tool for a broken bike, or a bandage for a scraped-up knee. Often, "Go in the house," signaled it was time to eat, or that it was getting close to bedtime. Every now and then, going in the house meant that there was a surprise waiting for me.

Now that I'm a parent, I find myself using this same phrase with my two children. I want to encourage someone who is dealing with an injustice after having done the right things. My encouragement to you today is to, "Go in the house".

What do I mean by, "Go in the house"? The house represents the place where God is. The house is a place of shelter. Just like as a child I found shelter from the rain in my parents' house, I can find shelter from the storms of life in the presence of God. The house is place of comfort. The bandage and medicine I needed for my scraped-up knee was located in the house. The balm and the soothing touch I need for my wounded heart or broken spirit are found in the presence of God. The house is also a place of nourishment. When it was time to eat growing up, I would go in the house to eat my dinner. Likewise, when my hungry soul needs to be fed, there is a feast spread before me in the presence of God. The house is a place of rest. In the same way I went in the house when it was bedtime as a child, I can go into the presence of God to experience rest from the cares of this life. And sometimes the house is a place of celebration.

More Than
We Can Bear

It was a frigid Christmas Eve, and I was at home preparing to go to our Christmas Eve church service. At the last minute I decided not to go. This was a very unusual decision for me, but I felt an uneasiness in my spirit that I really couldn't explain at the time. My wife and kids went to church without me. As I walked through the kitchen I noticed a plastic shopping bag on the kitchen counter my wife had brought home from the store earlier that afternoon. I innocently thought, "I wonder what she bought," and looked in. I was not trying to spy on her or anything like that. After all, it was a shopping bag sitting on the kitchen counter in plain view. Inside there were some sampler boxed chocolates, a bag of snack-sized Snickers, and some bags of nuts. There was also a greeting card. I read the card, and the words were very romantic. Immediately my heart sank. My first thought was this card couldn't be for me. My wife was barely speaking to me at the time, and had been treating me with contempt. I knew the candy wasn't for her, because she only ate chocolate during her menstrual cycle, and this wasn't her time. I decided to wait and see if she would give me that card the following morning for Christmas. I prayed she would. I thought maybe my wife would use Christmas as a starting point to renew our struggling relationship.

Soon after my wife returned home from church, the shopping bag disappeared. By then I was sure she hadn't planned on leaving it out on the counter, regardless of whom the items were for. That night I didn't sleep well at all. I kept looking over at the clock next to my bed. The time seemed to creep by. While I lay in my bed, I kept praying that my wife would give me that card in the morning. I wanted my marriage to work, and I didn't want to believe the worst.

On Christmas morning we exchanged and unwrapped dozens of gifts. After all the gifts were opened, there was nothing for me—not even from the kids, through my wife. (They were too young to buy gifts on their own, being only four and two years old.) Then after seeing that I was the only one empty-handed, my wife pointed to a small gift bag the size of an index card and said to me, "This is for you." It appeared that she had not expected me to give her any gifts, and felt she had to make up for the fact she had not gotten me anything. In the bag was one of those boxes of chocolate I had seen the previous day, out of the wrapper, (she had to remove the wrapper to separate them), one bag of nuts, and about 4 mini Snickers bars. No card.

I was heart-broken. My wife was a gift-giver. She enjoyed spending money on gifts for others. In the past, she had given me a camcorder, a scanner, nice shirts and the like. So for her to give me a couple of pieces of candy and some nuts as a

Christmas present was a significant statement. That was just like giving me nothing at all.

In what seemed like an effort to cover, she said she had gotten me a gift card from one of the big electronics stores, but it must have gotten lost under the Christmas tree. That was an obvious lie, but I let it go. How could it get lost under the tree? It would be easy enough to find. Then she changed her story to say that maybe she lost it in her car, but she never went to her car to look for it. To this day I haven't received the gift card. It was not the gifts themselves that were the issue for me. I have been known to give gifts back to her and tell her that she didn't need to spend that kind of money on me. I knew what this meant. My Christmas gift was the knowledge and confirmation that my wife was having an affair.

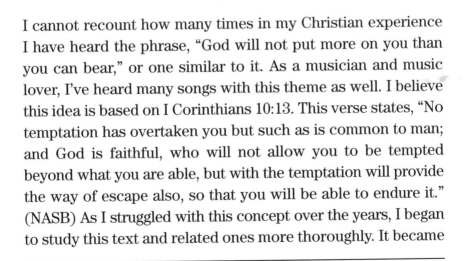

I cannot recount how many times in my Christian experience I have heard the phrase, "God will not put more on you than you can bear,"

I cannot recount how many times in my Christian experience I have heard the phrase, "God will not put more on you than you can bear," or one similar to it. As a musician and music lover, I've heard many songs with this theme as well. I believe this idea is based on I Corinthians 10:13. This verse states, "No temptation has overtaken you but such as is common to man; and God is faithful, who will not allow you to be tempted beyond what you are able, but with the temptation will provide the way of escape also, so that you will be able to endure it." (NASB) As I struggled with this concept over the years, I began to study this text and related ones more thoroughly. It became clear to me that I Corinthians 10:13 is referring to temptations and not trials and burdens. I discovered through scripture that God absolutely does at times allow us to experience more than we can bear, because it is not His intention for us to bear it—or bear it alone. I Peter 5:7 admonishes us to "(cast) our cares upon Him because He cares for (us)." Matthew 11:28–30 suggests that the Lord wants us to exchange our burden for His, because His yoke is easy and burden is light. Even Jesus himself received help in bearing his physical cross on His way to Calvary.

The believer in Christ cannot escape all trials.

I received some opposition to this interpretation of I Corinthians 10:13 when I shared my viewpoint with other believers. It was suggested to me that the word trial could be interchanged with the word temptation in this text. The case was made that God indeed will not allow more trials than we can bear. The phrase in this text that made the point for me is, "but He… will provide the way of escape." The believer in Christ cannot escape all trials. James makes this point clear in his letter. Peter also reiterates this point. (I Peter 4:12) We don't have to give in to temptation, but there is no escaping the trials of life. In fact, we should expect them.

Paul testified in his second letter to the Corinthian church that while he and his companions were in Asia, they were burdened excessively, beyond their strength. That means it was more than they could bear. It was so much so that he states they despaired even of life. (2 Corinthians 1:8) Paul explained that this "sentence of death" occurred that they would not trust in themselves, but in God. God wants us to trust Him, and He often uses trials to facilitate that trust. I would also submit that every burden we are carrying was not put on us by God. Sometimes we create our own loads. Sometimes other people place burdens on us, as when King Saul tried to put his heavy armor on young David.

> *I was thrust into the depths of anguish at a level I had never experienced or could ever have imagined. It was more than I could bear.*

I wish I could say the pain ended there on Christmas morning with the realization of my wife's infidelity. I wish I could say there was immediate repentance, forgiveness, and beginning of the restoration process. That was not the case. I was thrust into the depths of anguish at a level I had never experienced or could ever have imagined. It was more than I could bear. I truly got in touch with the term "heartache". I lost weight—something I could not afford to do. I was depressed. Some days it took all the strength I had just to get out of bed in the morning.

When you're going through a difficult time, the last thing you want to hear from someone is, "God wouldn't put more on you than you can bear." The implication is, "Why are you responding that way? You can handle it."

Whether or not one agrees with my thesis, I think we would all agree that when we are engulfed in difficulty, it often *feels* like it is more than we can bear—even if we can indeed bear it.

Principles

The Word of God teaches us that we will reap whatever we have sown in our lives. (Galatians 6:7–9). This text is often referred to in the negative context, but this principle applies to the good and the bad we do. If we sow seeds of kindness and love, we should expect to reap the same in return. If, on the other hand, we plant seeds of hatred and discord, we should not be surprised when hatred and discord return to us.

I must point out that everything that we go through in life is not a harvest. Jesus made that clear in John 9:3 with the man who was born blind. Jesus stated that this man's blindness was so that God could be glorified, not because he or his parents had sinned. It seems unfair that this man would have to suffer for so many years in this condition for no fault of his own. We don't have to plant weeds—they come up all by themselves. Sometimes we don't understand why we go through the things that we do. The reason for our circumstance could be solely that God might get the glory from it. We have to remember that it's not about us. We are here for a purpose that is bigger than ourselves.

One of the truths about harvesting is that there is some-times crop failure! (Jeremiah 12:13) Praise God that some of the bad seeds we plant get choked out by weeds. I'm thankful that sometimes the sun scorches our bad seedlings, or frost destroys the harmful plants that have sprouted. The principle of mercy is sometimes applied to our situation, where God does not give us the consequences we deserve. We know we deserve to be in jail right now for some of the things we've done in our past, but God has been merciful and not allowed us to face the full impact of our consequences.

Sometimes the increase is small, while other times there is a boom crop. If we had known that one act would have caused so much damage, we would have made different choices. The "weather conditions" or our environment also play a role. If the crop is fed and nourished, it is more likely to produce, whereas a drought or flood will destroy it.

> ...*one seed of kindness can have far-reaching effects.*

Another truth about harvesting is that you reap more than what you sow. This is good news on the positive side. One kernel of corn produces a stalk with many ears of corn, which supply many more kernels. In the same way, one seed of kindness can have far-reaching effects. One loving deed can produce years of favor. At the same token, we can find ourselves reaping years of pain because of one careless act.

A third reality about harvesting is that you reap at a later time than when you plant. The crop does not come up immediately. A farmer doesn't return to his field the day after he plants it looking for a harvest. It takes time for it to produce. There is a process that must take place. Just because you don't see fruit right away does not mean fruit is not coming. In the positive sense, we must sometimes be patient for our crop to come in. We may be tempted to give up too quickly, but we have to wait. On the negative side, we should not be fooled into thinking that we will not suffer the consequences of our sin just because the consequences have not yet happened. A day of accountability is coming! How often have we thought we've gotten away with something, only to be exposed some time much later?

We believe God's principle of sowing and reaping is true, so we question why things are turning out the way they are.

We tend to think that the reward we receive for our actions will be in the same category as our actions, but that may not always be the case. You may be one who gives generously financially to those in need. It is reasonable to think that the blessing you receive from your giving will be financial in nature. However, it may not be. God may choose to bless you by keeping you in good health, or providing you with peace in a challenging situation. We may not even be aware at the time that we are reaping at that moment.

> *God may choose to bless you by keeping you in good health, or providing you with peace in a challenging situation.*

While I was single, and before I met my future wife, I had an experience in which a married woman from my church wanted to have a sexual affair with me while her husband was out of town on business. She was a believer as well. I had previously had a few innocent conversations with her at church related to music. From those few conversations, and her perception of me from afar, she became emotionally attached to me. After a while she shared with me the emptiness she felt in her marriage. Her husband was not there for her emotionally. I was a listening ear for her, not realizing what I was setting myself up for. She was emotionally unstable, and her perceptions became distorted. I was totally surprised on the day she propositioned me for sex. She had made all the arrangements, and all I had to do was show up. I was not interested for many reasons, and turned down her request. She pursued me for a little while after that, but I stood my ground. She eventually recognized how wrong this would be, and began refocusing on her own marriage.

I expected that since I did not sin against another man's wife in this way that the same would not happen to me. After all, the principle of reaping and sowing applies to the positive as well as the negative. It seemed that my reward for my integrity was to lose my wife to an adulterous affair. Knowing how I had responded when faced with the opportunity to sin against another man's wife made my wife's adultery even more painful for me. I could have understood it better if I had done the same thing previously myself. Then I would be reaping what I had sown. I struggled with why God would allow this particular set of circumstances to occur. My hurt was magnified when I learned of an additional person my wife had an inappropriate relationship with during our marriage. He was someone I trusted, and who should have been looking out for my family's well-being. Instead he took advantage of a situation that was presented to him.

The Bible tells the story of Jacob and Laban in Genesis chapters 29–31. Jacob had fallen in love with Laban's younger daughter, Rachel, who was a beautiful woman. Jacob agreed to work for seven years for Laban in exchange for his daughter, Rachel, in marriage. After Jacob worked the seven years, Laban deceived Jacob and gave him his other daughter, Leah, instead. Laban then changed the agreement, and required Jacob to work another seven years for Rachel, which he did. Also, when it came to their livestock, Jacob said that Laban had cheated him and changed his wages ten times. Jacob also faced resentment from Laban's sons. They felt Jacob had become wealthy by taking the livestock that belonged to their father.

The Lord vindicated Jacob by allowing only his livestock to mate and reproduce, and not Laban's. Jacob was blessed tremendously. Laban's attitude was no longer friendly toward Jacob. In Genesis 31:12b, God comforted Jacob with the words, "I have seen all that Laban has been doing to you." I inserted my wife's name in place of Laban in this verse. It became a source of encouragement to me throughout this ordeal. It was a comforting reminder that God was aware of my situation. It gave me hope that He would one day rectify the situation for me as He did for Jacob. God told Jacob in verse three, "I will be with you." I claimed that promise as well.

Peace

For many months I prayed for a miracle to occur in my marriage. I prayed that the relationship would be restored. I loved my wife and wanted to be with her. Our relationship was deficient, but I believed it could improve. Although the miracle I prayed for did not happen, a miracle occurred nevertheless. The miracle was the peace that God supernaturally supplied to me in the midst of this trying ordeal I was experiencing. This was the greatest period of darkness I had ever encountered. Still, I had a sense that somehow He was going to bring me through this situation, although I couldn't see it. I remarked to several people that the miracle was simply the fact that I was sitting there having a conversation with them. I was in touch with my own weaknesses well enough to know that I could have easily reacted in a way that would have caused me to end up in jail. I could have allowed anger to make me do something I would regret. Another possibility was that I could have lost my mind. Instead, God gave me peace. Family members and even those who counseled me were amazed at how I handled the onslaught of weapons that were thrust at me. They admitted that had they been in my shoes, they would not have been so calm. I was quick to give the credit to the Lord, because I knew myself, and what I was capable of doing. Once again, I was experiencing the keeping power of God. God's peace really does surpass all understanding.

> *Sometimes it seemed my choices played right into the hands of those who were against me.*

God had to give me peace with decisions I had to make. They would not be easy to make, and most likely, not well received. The decisions would not be understood by everyone affected, or even those looking on. I hated that fact because it made me look really bad at times. Sometimes it seemed my choices played right into the hands of those who were against me. I wished others could understand my motives. Many of the choices would have long-term effects. Sometimes even the outcome of those decisions was the opposite of what I desired or expected, but I had to follow what I believed to be God's leading.

God also gave me peace with the past. I have the assurance that I have been forgiven. Mistakes were made in the past, but I could not dwell on them. I had to move forward. I would not allow my failures to cripple me. In the end, I did the best I could in the situation I was in. I couldn't undo certain actions. I couldn't take back certain words. I had to accept the consequences.

Miracle

I am reminded of the story of the little girl who prayed for rain in the middle of a hot, dry summer. Believing that God would answer her prayer, she carried her umbrella with her. Again, this required faith. Can you imagine how strange this girl looked carrying an umbrella where there was no prospect of rain? She could not be concerned with what others thought of her. She fully expected that it would rain, so she acted upon that expectation. She put her faith into action. We must live as if we truly believe God is going to do what we are asking Him for. James tells us that if we don't, we are a double-minded man who is unstable. (James 1:6–8) I attempted to put this principle into practice in my own life. For example, I continued to wear my wedding ring as an act of faith, believing that God would restore my marriage, even after my wife and I were separated. I felt that if I took it off, I would be accepting the idea that my marriage was over. My circumstances indicated one thing, but faith told a different story. I didn't act as though I wasn't married just because my wife wasn't present.

> *My circumstances indicated one thing, but faith told a different story.*

I could look back over my life and recall instances where the Lord has worked out a situation like only He can. That gave me hope that He would do it again. One of the most noteable instances was the restoration of my marriage after my wife and I were separated the first time. My wife and I had been apart for ten months. We had very little communication with each other during that time, mainly due to a restraining order she filed against me. My wife had researched the divorce option. The longer we were apart, the worse the situation became. As the months progressed, there appeared to be no hope that we would ever get back together, but God answered prayer in a mighty way. He brought us back together and allowed us to move on.

Through all of the trials, I never doubted God's ability to answer my prayer, but I did wonder whether or not He was willing. I couldn't understand why He wouldn't be. I later learned that God is often willing, but He does not force His will onto us. In the case of a marriage, if one party is not willing to follow God's plan, it doesn't matter what the willing party says or does. It takes both persons to make it work. I knew what I was praying for was according to God's Word, yet it was still not to be. I wanted God to orchestrate the situation so that my marriage would stay in tact. I wanted Him to intervene so my wife's actions and attitude would change. To my disappointment, that did not happen.

No Guarantees

Often in the movies and on television, stories have a happy ending—the good guys win out. In real life, there is not always a happy ending to every story. I searched for a biblical example of a person who did the right thing, yet the outcome proved to be unfavorable. There was the obvious example of Job, but I knew I was no Job. Though he suffered great losses, in the end, Job received back double what he lost.

Joseph was another candidate. (Genesis 37, Genesis 39–47) The case could be argued that Joseph didn't necessarily do the right thing in all cases. His pride may have been the reason for some of his predicament, though maybe not in the case of Potiphar's wife. Still again, Joseph's end proved to be a great blessing. He became second in command of Egypt.

That brought me to consider Stephen in the New Testament. Stephen was stoned for preaching the gospel. (Acts 7:57–60) His reward for obedience to God was death.

I was not a martyr, and my situation was not about being persecuted for my faith.

I began to be encouraged by the fact that my search was coming up empty. I asked myself, could the fact that I could find very few examples mean that God really does reward His children who seek to follow Him and obey His commandments? That doesn't mean that things will work out the way I think they should, but God will ultimately cause all things to work together for my good. (Romans 8:28) There are no formulas that we can plug in and get a desired result. What works for the guy on the other pew may not work for me. Some situations will not be worked out until we get to heaven.

> *There are no formulas that we can plug in and get a desired result.*

Job wanted relief from his suffering, but God's plan called for him to wait. Joseph did not want to be confined to that dungeon for those years, but the Lord saw fit to keep him there. I'm sure Stephen would not have chosen the excruciating pain of being pelted by large rocks, yet God chose to call him home that way. I had to face the fact that heaven could be the place where vindication would take place for me, and not earth.

After I had nearly given up my search for a biblical model to illustrate this point, God showed me what I thought was an unlikely example in Luke 15:25–32. This text is the account of the prodigal son. My subject turned out to be the prodigal son's older brother. In this older son, I began to see an example of a man who was faithful in doing good, yet the circumstances did not turn out the way he desired.

The story of the prodigal son is a very familiar one. Jesus told the story of a man who had two sons. The younger son asked his father for his inheritance before his father died. The father divided his wealth among both sons. When the younger son received his portion, he went away to a far country and wasted his money on wild living. He then encountered a famine, and was nearly starving. After being relegated to feeding pigs, he realized that his father had enough resources back at home. The son decided to return home and ask his father to make him one of his hired servants.

As he made his way home, his father saw him a long way off. He ran to him, kissed him and received him home. He told his servants to put a robe on his back, a ring on his finger, and sandals on his feet. The dad instructed them to kill the fattened calf, and prepare a feast to celebrate the return of his lost son.

For centuries in the church, the older son in this parable has been criticized for his response to his brother's return, but to some extent, his anger is understandable. What I began to see in this son is not the portrayal we in the church have often heard over the years of this brother. We hear of his jealousy and bitter spirit. We are told of his sinful behavior. I believe that if we could get in touch with the reasons for his responses, we may not be so hard on this son. We would have to acknowledge how similar our own hearts have been at various junctures in our lives.

It is interesting how we take a glimpse or snapshot of this man's life, and characterize his whole life in a negative way. Suppose just one day in our life would forever define our character in the minds of those who observe us. That is a very convicting thought. Actually for me, one incident has defined who I am in some people's eyes, but I thank God that He sees the sum total of my life, and evaluates me on the basis of who I am in Christ.

The Bible does not give us a name for this son in our story. It only says that a certain man had two sons. Since this is the older son, I will call him "Junior."

Let's take a look at the character of this older son. First of all, we see that Junior honored his father. In contrast to his younger brother, he did not dishonor his father by asking for his inheritance while he was still alive. That would have been disrespectful. His younger brother was essentially saying, "Dad, I can't wait for you to die." As the eldest son, he had the rights of inheritance, but he did not exercise them. Junior received his inheritance at the same time as his brother. He could have gone away as well, but he stayed with his father. He was an honorable son who cared about his father. We could use more sons like him today.

Secondly, he was faithful. Junior served his father faithfully for years, never neglecting a command. He did everything his father asked him to do. He was even in the field working on the day his wayward brother returned home. The text intimates that he worked long hours in the field, because the preparations had already been made and the festivities underway when he returned to the house. There were no microwave ovens and convenience stores in those days, so it took time to prepare the meal and the gathering.

Next, we find that Junior possessed the quality of humility. He had authority as the son of the master. The parable says he summoned one of the servants and began inquiring. Even though he had authority, he humbled himself as a servant. The text states earlier that the father had many hired servants, so it was not necessary for this son to work, yet it appears he chose to do so. The attribute of servanthood is one that the scriptures teach that all believers should possess. We have the example of Christ himself, as pointed out in Philippians 2:5–8. He humbled himself as a servant. In Mark 10:43–44, Jesus states that "whoever wishes to become great among you shall be your servant; and whoever wishes to be first among you shall be slave to all." I submit that Junior was not such a bad guy. Some of us may even owe this son an apology.

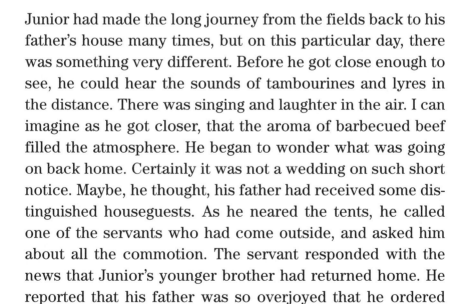

In Mark 10:43–44, Jesus states that "whoever wishes to become great among you shall be your servant; and whoever wishes to be first among you shall be slave to all."

Junior had made the long journey from the fields back to his father's house many times, but on this particular day, there was something very different. Before he got close enough to see, he could hear the sounds of tambourines and lyres in the distance. There was singing and laughter in the air. I can imagine as he got closer, that the aroma of barbecued beef filled the atmosphere. He began to wonder what was going on back home. Certainly it was not a wedding on such short notice. Maybe, he thought, his father had received some distinguished houseguests. As he neared the tents, he called one of the servants who had come outside, and asked him about all the commotion. The servant responded with the news that Junior's younger brother had returned home. He reported that his father was so overjoyed that he ordered that the fattened calf be killed, and a great feast be prepared to celebrate the joyous event.

This news did not sit well with Junior. He became angry when he received the explanation for the music and dancing he heard when he approached the house that particular day. I do not believe he was angered by the return of his brother, for that was a good thing. It was the perceived unfairness of his brother's treatment compared to his own, that triggered this response. Anyone who has siblings can certainly relate to this situation. I remember how I felt as a boy when my brother or sister received something that I didn't. While anger itself is not a sin, this son's anger was misplaced because the fact that his father had thrown a feast for his wayward brother was not a sin. The father had the right to do what he wanted with his resources.

> *Are we angry because a sin has been committed against us, or is it merely because an expectation has not been met?*

Anger is a secondary emotion. When we are angry, we should examine the cause of the anger to determine if it is justified. Are we angry because a sin has been committed against us, or is it merely because an expectation has not been met? It's not a sin if your wife doesn't cook. It's not a sin for your husband to forget your anniversary.

It is still understandable why this son felt this way. How many times in our own experiences have we seen situations in which people who have done wrong seem to be rewarded for their actions? We follow all the rules, yet the person who cheats and schemes gets the promotion. The drug dealer down the street is living extravagantly, while we struggle to pay our bills every month. Even throughout the Psalms, the psalmist struggled with the seeming reward of the wicked. Let's face it; life is often unfair.

Junior desired the earthly, tangible recognition from his father for his service to him. He wanted to be honored among his friends—something that had never happened before. That, in itself, was not necessarily a sinful desire. The father's response to his angry son was, "you have always been with me, and all that is mine is yours." (v. 31)

This response did not appear to be adequate for Junior. If we are honest with ourselves, we also often seek the earthly, tangible recognition of our heavenly Father. That desire is not wrong unless our motivation for our service is the recognition. The knowledge that we are His children and heirs of His promise does not always remove the hurt and emptiness when we feel unappreciated. We want something that we can see or touch.

I believe there are three things we can learn from the older son in this text when we have done the right thing yet the outcome is unfavorable. Number one, we must engage our Father in prayer. This is not a "now I lay me down to sleep" prayer, but a heart-to-heart exchange between oneself and God. One of the definitions Webster gives us for the word engage is to induce to participate. It's okay to ask God the tough questions. He can handle them. I did some serious praying during my time of crisis.

I personally appreciate the honestly of this son. He told his father exactly what was bothering him. He didn't hold back. We have a heavenly Father who is big enough to handle our honest complaint. He already knows our every thought anyway, yet He desires to hear from us. When we come to God with honesty and sincerity, we place ourselves in position for Him to work on our behalf. Not only is prayer talking with God, it is also listening to hear what God has to say to us. It is a dialog, or two-way conversation. Junior had to listen to his father's response as well.

Was it too much for Junior to ask for a party for all the years of faithful service to his father? Would he have to wait until heaven to receive his reward? Does this son's desire indicate that his motivation for his actions was temporal recognition? Was his desire sinful? These are some thought-provoking questions.

There are similar questions we must ask ourselves. If I faithfully tithe for 20 years, should I expect God to bless me to the extent that I am not in want for my daily sustenance?

We may not always admit it, but we have certain expectations in life.

We may not always admit it, but we have certain expectations in life. If we are faithful to our spouse, and the vows we made before God, we expect our spouse to be faithful to us. If we do all that is required of us on the job—and more, we expect the recognition from our boss. If we obey the speed limit and all the traffic rules when driving, we expect to make it safely to our destination. If we teach our children right and wrong, we expect that they won't end up in jail or on drugs, etc.

I knew a Christian man who never smoked cigarettes or worked in a dirty factory, but he died of lung cancer. He was in his forties, and left behind a family. We have to be careful, though, not to act as if God owes us something because of our good deeds.

We must submit to the sovereignty of God. He is in control. He can do what He wants to, when He wants to, and how He wants to. We may never see the fruit of our labor in this lifetime. That was never promised to us. There are no guarantees. We can rest assured, however, that the Lord sees, and He will reward us in due time. (I Corinthians 15:58, Galatians 6:9) Also, God will ultimately get the glory out of our lives.

In many ways I was like this older brother in our parable. I compared myself to others around me. I knew of husbands who were involved in many sinful activities. They beat their wives, neglected their family responsibilities, etc. These men still had marriages and families that were intact. My circumstances seemed unfair. I certainly made many mistakes in my marriage, but I was faithful to my wife. I provided for my family... I felt I deserved to have a fattened calf killed for me.

Like Junior, I had done the right things. I had been faithful yet the reward seemed to be elusive. I found myself in the midst of a set of circumstances that I did not like. Like this older son, I felt slighted. I watched people around me commit sin with no apparent consequences. In fact, they appeared to be rewarded for their actions. They had a feast prepared for them and were given gifts. I assessed my own good deeds and questioned what I had to show for them. Honestly, I felt I deserved better. This was not the way things were supposed to turn out in my estimation. I was supposed to grow old with my wife. I was supposed to spend all the holidays with my family. I wasn't supposed to only see my kids on weekends and during the summer.

A Walk of Faith

Sometimes in life there are no answers and no direction. There are times when God gives us clear direction before we embark on our journey. Other times He requires that we first move, then He provides instructions along the way, as was the case with Abraham (Genesis 12:1, Hebrews 11:8). Abraham did not know where he was going when he left his hometown of Ur, but he had to follow God's leading. God just told Abraham to go.

I was often frustrated by Christian leaders who would give the impression (and made statements) that every decision they made has been preceded by a clear direction from God. They would quote the verse of scripture that says, "My sheep hear my voice and follow me..." They would imply that if you could not hear God's voice in every decision, there was something wrong with your relationship with God. I knew in my own life, that sometimes there were no signs for me to go by. There was no fleece, as was the case with Gideon (Judges 6:36–38). Sometimes I've had to make a decision and trust that it was the right one. Sometimes it was not confirmed until a later time. There were also other biblical examples of godly men who received no sign or clear direction.

If we could always see, there would be no reason to trust God.

The Bible is clear that this Christian journey of ours is a walk of faith. (Hebrews 11:6) If we could always see, there would be no reason to trust God. Life often brings us tests to reveal how much we depend on Him. They are not meant to destroy us, but to approve us. The Lord wants us to pass the tests. Through our tests we may discover that our faith is lacking. The tests give us opportunities to build our faith.

I have personally had to learn to trust God beyond all hope. At times I have not understood where God was taking me, or why, but I had to trust Him. It is easy to talk about trust, but it is a whole other thing to put it into practice in a difficult situation. Proverbs 3:5–6 have been favorite verses of mine from a child, but it has often been difficult applying these verses to my personal life. In these verses, Solomon urges us to trust in the Lord with all of our heart, not just a part. Then, we are not to rely on our own comprehension of the situation. I certainly didn't understand all the reasons for my circumstance, and that made it much more difficult to trust. It's not easy to trust God with everything that we have. (At least that's not the case for me.) Often times, our faith must be tested. God orchestrates situations in our lives that force us to prove the faith we say we have, and depend fully on Him. I am one of those people who likes to know what I am getting into beforehand. When available, I like to have as much information as possible. It's not easy for me to walk blindly into something without knowing all the facts. I like to analyze the situation and try to make the best decision. This mindset often goes against faith. God sometimes calls me to move without knowing the outcome. My understanding does not compare to God's infinite wisdom and knowledge.

Foolish instructions

To Abraham, God said kill your son, Isaac, who was promised to be heir to a great nation. (Genesis 12:1–13.) These instructions couldn't have made sense to Abraham, yet he believed God.

The Lord told Joshua to command the Israelites to march around the walls of Jericho for six days. On the seventh day, they were to march around the walls, blow trumpets, and shout. (Joshua 6:1–21) How strange they must have looked to the people of Jericho. I can hear them asking, "what in the world are these people doing?" After God's people obeyed His command, the walls of Jericho fell flat, and the Israelites destroyed the city. I'm sure the people could not have anticipated this outcome.

Elisha, the prophet of God, told Naaman to wash in the Jordan river seven times to cure his leprosy. (2 Kings 5:10) How could dipping in some water cure leprosy? Naaman himself asked, "Why the dirty Jordan river, instead of one of the cleaner rivers in Damascus?" These instructions did not make sense.

These are just a few examples in the Bible of what seem to be foolish instructions from God. In all three cases, it was the man's obedience to God that made the difference. They obeyed God and He worked through their obedience. Isaac's life was spared, Jericho was destroyed, and Naaman's leprosy was cured.

God wants us to trust Him, and no one, or nothing else.

Sometimes God will tell us to do something that seems absolutely crazy. It just makes no sense to us. God wants us to trust Him, and no one, or nothing else. Sometimes the thing He tells us to do seems to be just the opposite of what we are seeking. I had to let go of the woman I loved, and the relationship I was trying so desperately to hold on to...

I fully believed God had given her to me just as He gave Isaac to Abraham. Like Naaman, I didn't understand the process he was taking me through to get to my healing. Surely there had to be a better way. But, like the Israelites when facing Jericho, I had to follow God's instructions and go through the process. God's ways are not our ways... We cannot understand God.

> *The parent knows more than the child. We must submit to the sovereignty of God.*

The second principle I gather from Junior is that we must entrust ourselves to our Father's plan. The father replied to his son's objection in verse 32 by stating that "we had to be merry and rejoice, for this brother of yours was dead and has begun to live, and was lost and has been found." This son may not have understood it, but he had to accept the fact that it was his father's will to throw this party. His anger and disappointment clouded his vision. There was something going on that was bigger than what he could see. The same principle holds true for us. It's the difference between a child's perspective and a parent's. The parent knows more than the child. We must submit to the sovereignty of God. He is in control. He can do what He wants to do. His ways are higher than our ways.

God is a just God, and He will execute justice. Also, God will ultimately get the glory out of our lives. I'll admit it's not easy to entrust ourselves to the Father's plan, but we have to say, "yes, Lord, to Your will", even when it doesn't seem fair. It involves remembering God's work in the past on our behalf. If we take an honest look back over our lives we will recall how the Lord has brought us through many situations before. If He did it before, He can certainly do it again. I had to surrender my will to God's will.

Special Assignment

It was a warm, sunny June afternoon, just ten days after my 29th birthday. Around 200 of our family and friends gathered in the sanctuary of our church. Bridesmaids entered in their peach-colored dresses. I proceeded down the aisle in my ivory-colored tuxedo, accompanied by trumpet music I composed, to meet my beautiful bride, who made herself ready to receive me. You may think that this description is not the typical American wedding scenario, and you are correct. The church that my fiancée and I belonged to at that time often performed weddings in an unusual fashion. It was unusual for our culture, but very biblical. The wedding ceremony we chose was entitled, "The Bride of Christ." It depicted the biblical account of Jesus Christ, the bridegroom, and the Church, His bride, at the great wedding supper of the Lamb. Instead of the groom being in place beforehand and waiting for the bride to enter, my fiancée made her entrance first and waited for me to enter. She was dressed in a beautiful ivory gown as she entered the sanctuary to the sounds of a flute solo I had composed specifically for her entitled, *"A Child's Heart"*. Our pastor described the biblical account of the marriage supper of the Lamb from the book of Revelation. He even gave an invitation for the guests to receive Christ.

We exchanged rings, lit a unity candle, we took communion together as husband and wife, and then kissed.

Many of our wedding guests had never witnessed a wedding ceremony such as ours that modeled the biblical marriage ceremony. Some commented on how the ceremony impacted them. My wife and I agreed our wedding was a powerful display and that God was glorified through our ceremony. We recognized that Satan would try to attack us because of the great testimony that was demonstrated that day. The two of us had already agreed beforehand that divorce would not be an option for us. I had the confidence that even though we had difficulties, my wife would be committed to me and to her vows to the Lord. I trusted that she had the same confidence.

That day I promised to "take her to be my wife, to have and to hold, from this day forward; for better, for worse; for richer, for poorer; in sickness and in health; to love and to cherish until we are separated by death; as God is my witness." My fiancée made a similar promise to me.

I thank God that we belonged to a church that valued the marriage covenant, and sought to ensure that these vows were not taken lightly. I am especially grateful for the premarital counseling that my wife and I received. It was not just a half-hour session with the pastor a week before the wedding, as is the case in many churches I know of. Our church required at least ten months of counseling before a couple could get married at the church. The pastor who counseled us was a degreed, licensed marriage counselor. The sessions helped my wife and I discover issues before entering marriage that we could address and begin to work on. The counseling allowed us to examine our personality profiles, and understand how we impacted each other. There was training on communication and finances as well.

> *The counseling allowed us to examine our personality profiles, and understand how we impacted each other.*

To love my wife as Christ loves the church was a heavy challenge. I had big shoes to fill. One of my greatest challenges was determining when to require responsibility, as opposed to showing mercy. My natural tendency was to require responsibility and make people accountable for their actions. For example, I had an affinity for remembering small details of conversations we had, and point out incongruencies when the same issue came up later. (Now, different stresses have affected my recall, and I've learned that some of these little things don't matter anymore.) I would want my wife to stand behind what she had said, or explain what changed. I had to learn to show mercy. I had a high value for what was right.

My fiancée and I took the Meyers-Briggs Personality Type Inventory to assist us in discovering personality differences and similarities. We learned that the two of us were opposites in many ways, but that was not unusual. Opposites often attract. We gained better understanding of how we complimented each other. We used the *Taylor-Johnson Temperament Analysis* (TJTA) to measure our individual emotional and behavioral adjustments. Our counselor emphasized that if God called us together, He was not afraid of our differences, and we should not be either. The key was to make these differences work for us and not against us.

Our thirteen counseling sessions focused on the communication and conflict issues from our personality and value differences. At the conclusion, our counselor felt my wife and I had the tools necessary for quality communication and conflict resolution. He concluded that the potential for satisfaction was available if we applied the strategies we had learned during our sessions. His major area of prayer for us was that we could keep free from the buildup of negative assumptions.

The following seven assets were identified that we carried into the marriage:

- Commitment to Jesus Christ
- Honesty
- Intellectual Maturity
- Self-Discipline
- Persevering
- Financial Maturity
- Teachable Attitudes

Armed with that preparation, we embarked on a life of matrimony as Mr. and Mrs. Rodney A. Winters. I remember the first day I met my future wife. It was a hot Saturday afternoon in August, at our church's singles' picnic. She recently joined the church I attended. A fellow member of the congregation pointed her out to me the previous Sunday, after church, as someone I might be interested in dating. After looking at her, I told that person that she was not my type, and that I wasn't interested in her. I was very picky about what I was looking for. When I went to that picnic I was hoping that a particular young lady I was interested in would be there. I returned a day earlier from a trip just so I wouldn't miss the chance to interact with her outside of church. I was disappointed that she didn't show up. I took the opportunity to introduce myself to my future wife and a friend who was with her. We engaged in some playful banter. Onlookers immediately thought I was interested in her. It was really a response to the disappointment I was feeling since the other young lady did not attend. I felt I had nothing to lose and that it was low risk and it was an opportunity for me to talk to someone. Never would I have never guessed that two years later, we would be vowing to love each other "until death do us part".

> *Never would I have never guessed that two years later, we would be vowing to love each other "until death do us part".*

After the picnic, I asked for her telephone number, and we began a friendship. The friendship quickly developed into a close friendship, but there was no romantic interest. She made it clear to me that I was not her type as well. My listening skills and empathy that ignited the friendship so I believed. We talked on the telephone for hours and hours. She began to share with me very personal things about her life. I had a deep sense of compassion for her and wanted to give myself to her. As time went on, I began to see not only an inner beauty, but I was attracted to her physically as well. She has a photograph that was taken the same day I first saw her in the church foyer. When I see that picture, I wonder what was wrong with me that day that I didn't see her natural attractiveness. The relationship grew, and I began to love her and eventually knew that

I wanted to marry her. I knew I loved her because I wanted to give to her. She had the qualities I was looking for in a wife. We shared similar goals in life. Even at this point she still was not interested in a romantic relationship with me. I wondered how our friendship could remain so strong with my feelings being what they were. I prayed for months that the Lord would bring us together if it was His will. At a time I was not expecting it, she revealed that she loved me as well, and we began a relationship. It took a little encouragement from one of her roommates, but she saw potential in me as a boyfriend.

The fact that I was not attracted to her when I initially met her was always a sore spot for her. She wasn't used to a man not being attracted to her. I guess she wanted to be pursued by a man who found her to be beautiful. I actually did by this time, but it wasn't the same for her. I viewed it as positive that we were friends first, and I was attracted to her inner beauty before anything else. The friendship allowed us to learn about each other without the pressures of a dating relationship.

I proposed to her on her 24th birthday. After some coaxing, I convinced her to let me take her out to dinner for her birthday. She had not been feeling well that day, so it was a hard sell. I made reservations at a very nice restaurant located inside of one of the local hotels. Our table overlooked a beautiful waterfall on the river. After a romantic dinner, I presented her with a fairly large gift-wrapped box. She opened the box to find another smaller box. Inside of it was a yet smaller box. She finally got to a ring box. She opened the ring box to find a diamond engagement ring I had picked out for her. "Will you marry me?" I asked. She was quite surprised and accepted my marriage proposal. Just then, people seated at other tables began to applaud. I had not realized that anyone had seen or heard what was taking place at our table. Caught up in the moment, I had forgotten that there were other people around. That was a happy day for me.

Our relationship had its ups and down. However, I viewed this as positive because I believed it gave us a realistic view of what marriage would be like. We would not always be in the honeymoon stage. Everything would not always be peaches and cream. Still I loved my fiancée very much and knew I wanted to spend the rest of my life with her. At one point, she returned the engagement ring, but it wasn't long before we were back together. I couldn't wait until we were husband and wife.

We began planning our wedding. My fiancée picked the colors for the dresses. We located a place for the reception. We considered dates. I was involved in the process, as we paid for the wedding ourselves.

Neither of us believed in long engagements. At our ages, we knew what we were looking for in a mate. There was no need to string things along.

We each brought our own issues into the marriage, but I was up for the challenge. Our honeymoon was great. The night of the wedding, we flew to New England to stay in a couple of bed-and-breakfasts for a week. We strolled the romantic beaches, shopped in the quaint boutiques, and of course enjoyed our first moments of sexual intimacy. All the years of waiting had come to an end. Our love for each other could be seen and felt. The week was not without its moments of comedy. It was a memorable experience.

Things started off well after we got home, but they quickly took a turn for the worse. We had returned to counseling before we reached our first anniversary. The honeymoon phase did not last long. I made some stupid mistakes in an effort to stand my ground against what I perceived as personal attacks against me. During an early argument my wife threatened to catch the next plane back to her mother's house. I called her bluff and she challenged me. I challenged back and told her I would call her mother and let her know to be waiting for her return. I didn't know my mother-in-law's phone number. My wife gave me the number and dared me to call. I did. Stupid!

Back then, I had a tendency to be critical. It was easy for me to point out faults in my wife. In fairness, I was and am more critical of myself than any other person. A lot of my self-criticism was internalized, so my wife did not know all of the details. I was not the best at giving compliments. When things were fine, I often wouldn't say anything. The thinking was that if everything is okay, nothing needs to be said. I didn't grow up hearing a lot of compliments. It took some time for me to learn to give affirmation.

> *The thinking was that if everything is okay, nothing needs to be said. I didn't grow up hearing a lot of compliments. It took some time for me to learn to give affirmation.*

Although financial maturity was one of the seven assets identified by our counseling pastor, my wife and I had issues related to money. During one of our many conversations before we even were engaged, she shared with me that she had a medical bill that she could not pay. The creditor had been hounding her. She was a struggling graduate student at the time, and didn't have much income, other than a part-time job after classes. At that point I knew I was going to ask her to marry me, although she did not know. We had talked a great deal about marriage, so I was confident she would accept my proposal. The way I looked at it, when we were married her debts would eventually be my debts anyway. I knew she didn't have the resources to fully pay me back, but I expected to be repaid some of it before we were married.

She did not know exactly how much the bill was, but I offered to pay it anyway. I signed a blank check and gave it to her. I was shocked when the check cleared to discover how much the check was written for. She was taking a big gamble that I had that kind of money in my checking account. I couldn't imagine even her family members giving her that amount of money. Fortunately, there were enough funds to cover the check. I chalked it up as a learning experience for me for writing a blank check. And as I had already reasoned, her debt would eventually be mine. However, I kept this incident in the back of my mind. We did not have a set repayment agreement.

As time went on, I never received any payments, although I watched her spend money on things that I considered to be frivolous. She also had a habit of buying nice gifts. I am not a gift person. They don't mean much to me. In terms of love languages, "gifts" is probably on the bottom for me. On special days, she bought me gifts that I thought were too expensive. I would have rather she had given me a loan payment with that money.

On my birthday she even borrowed money from her mother so that she could take me to an expensive restaurant and buy a nice gift. I appreciated the effort and sentiment, but that was not necessary for me. I am a simple guy who would have just as well enjoyed dinner at a less expensive restaurant. She also bought me a bottle of designer cologne. I had a sample of this cologne, and she liked how it smelled on me. I had told her previously that I didn't like it because I thought it was too strong. Again, I am a low-key person. Yet, I unwrapped the box she handed me to find this same cologne. She bought it because she liked it. I knew how much it cost, and thought it was a waste of money. I told her she should take it back. She apparently saw this as rejection, and appeared to take this very personally. In hindsight, I would have accepted the cologne and worn it proudly.

As our wedding date drew closer, I questioned my fiancée's integrity with regards to this loan issue. With the exception of her dress and a few small items, I paid for the entire wedding and honeymoon with my money.

During the course of the wedding preparation, my fiancée informed me of a wedding tradition that I was not aware of. She told me that the bride and groom are supposed to exchange gifts. I knew we would receive gifts from our guests, but I never knew I needed to buy a gift for my bride. I purchased a gold necklace and pendant for her. I had no idea what she was going to give me.

The day before the wedding as I struggled with the fact that I had not received one dime of the loan payment, I hoped my wife would give me just a small payment as her wedding gift to me. It wasn't the money that was the issue for me, but the principle. I remember thinking, "If she would just give me $20, that would mean the world to me." I imagined she would say, "Rodney, I know I can't pay you back the entire amount, but I just wanted to give you this token to say that I appreciate you lending me this money when no one else would." I did not want to think that I had been used by the woman I was about to marry in less than 24 hours.

Growing up in the church, I had always been taught that there was a special blessing for a marriage in which the husband and wife kept themselves pure sexually before the wedding. I was 29 years old when I got married, and a virgin. I did not view that as a small feat. There had been opportunities over the years to engage in sexual intercourse, but I always wanted to do what was right is God's sight. The peer pressure throughout the years was intense. The ridicule for not participating in the "locker room talk" was painful. I didn't have stories to tell about my sexual escapades. The assumption sometimes by others that I must be gay was hard to deal with. It was only by God's grace that I was able to accomplish this.

I must admit that I crossed the line of acceptable physical contact a number of times with my then fiancée, but we never engaged in sexual intercourse. The temptation to sin was great, especially when we knew we were getting married. It was easy to rationalize that we would be married soon, and give in to the temptation. I thank God that He preserved us until our wedding night. That was a testimony.

Our counselor and books we read warned us not to be disappointed if we didn't actually consummate the marriage on our wedding night. They said it was not uncommon for this to happen. They said that couples are often too exhausted after all the stresses of the wedding day to engage in sex on that night. They said the first marital sex is often on the day after the wedding. I remember thinking, "That would just be my luck to be a 'married virgin.'"

We landed at the airport that night at our interim destination and checked into our hotel. We got on the bed and I proceeded to approach my new bride. Sure enough, she didn't want to have sex. I was so hurt. I don't know if she was having flashbacks or if she was just too tired. All I could think of were all the times before we got married that she wanted to have sex, and I said we should wait. Now we were husband and wife, and she didn't want to have sex.

> *All I could think of were all the times before we got married that she wanted to have sex, and I said we should wait. Now we were husband and wife, and she didn't want to have sex.*

My next thought was to make the best of the situation. I was not going to let anything spoil our special day. I have waited 29 years, so I could wait another day. I thought, "This would be a good time to exchange our gifts," so I went and got the gift box I'd wrapped. I gave her the box and she opened the necklace. She seemed very pleased, and thanked me. I waited for my gift from her, but she hadn't gotten me one. This whole thing was her idea. I didn't know anything about this tradition until she told me.

The gift seemed to trigger something in her, and she said she wanted to have sex. So I didn't remain a virgin on my wedding night after all. I believed that the Lord was going to honor my faithfulness to this particular commandment by allowing me to experience a sexually fulfilling marriage. My future wife and I were very aware of certain issues from the past that would negatively affect our intimate relationship, yet there was the expectation that we would have a positive sex life. We had talked in depth about this issue. We even discussed how often we each expected to have intercourse once we got married. The topic was covered in our premarital counseling sessions. Neither of our expectations seemed unrealistic.

I could never have imagined the pain of rejection I would experience in this area. After my wife and I were married, it was not uncommon to go months without having sex. For me, having sex was one of the major anticipated benefits of getting married. Going to bed at night was often a painful experience for me. As I got in the bed and pulled the covers over me, I would wonder if tonight would be the night. If that particular night happened to be the one where there was intercourse, it was a bittersweet experience. I would know that there would be another long stretch of time before this would occur again. I tried to just enjoy the moment. I also knew that my wife did not enjoy the experience. She would tell me she felt an obligation to perform at least sometimes. It was apparent that she would often try to hurry the process.

That was ironic to me. I would hear married women complain about their husband's quick performance. I desired to please her. For me it was not just about getting my own needs met. It was very painful to know that as a husband I was not pleasing to my wife. I would often stay up as late as I could to minimize the hours I would spend in the bed with my wife. I was naturally a night owl, and she was an early bird, so that worked out well. I greatly desired to be with my wife, but she was frequently unwilling. I accepted this neglect from my wife, believing I was being sensitive to her situation. I was so concerned about how she would perceive me. I didn't want her to classify me as one of those demanding husbands. Ultimately I think I lost her respect.

I allowed her to take advantage of my consideration. I believed sex should be pleasurable for both parties. I knew my wife valued the Word of God, so I would sometimes point out the scriptures that teach the spouse's obligation to each other.

She accused me of trying to bully her with the Bible. To my regret, I was too passive. In general, people do what they can get away with. My action of silence gave consent to my wife's action of neglect. In one conversation much later in the marriage, my wife told me I should have just "been a man" and told her what I wanted. She claimed she would have "performed" out of obligation, even though she wouldn't have been into it emotionally. I knew that wasn't true, plus I didn't want obligatory sex. I called her bluff the following day and was accused of spousal rape.

I have learned over the years that the one who loves the least in a relationship controls the relationship. My wife was definitely that one. The one who loves more is at the mercy of the other person. He or she is more willing to give in to the one who loves less, because they want the relationship to work at almost any cost. The "greater lover" will do things that he or she ordinarily wouldn't do in order to please their partner or avoid conflict. If this continues over long periods of time, resentment can build up due to feelings of being unappreciated.

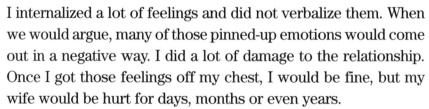

I have learned over the years that the one who loves the least in a relationship controls the relationship.

I internalized a lot of feelings and did not verbalize them. When we would argue, many of those pinned-up emotions would come out in a negative way. I did a lot of damage to the relationship. Once I got those feelings off my chest, I would be fine, but my wife would be hurt for days, months or even years.

Only two years into the marriage my wife and I went through a period of separation for ten months. Our daughter was only four months old. I was very disappointed with God. How could He allow me to go through such agony in this particular area of my life, when I waited 29 years to experience it? It was like having a prize, but not being able to hold it or experience it. I began to question if it was worth it for me to have maintained my sexual purity all those years. There are no guarantees. Though I took responsibility for my part in the event that led to the separation, I did not believe I deserved the outcome that followed. I felt I was treated worse by my wife than the persons that had truly harmed her.

I did not expect the long separation period that followed. I thought the situation would be a learning experience for my wife and I, and help us develop a better relationship. Instead, it drove a wedge between the two of us. She made it known that she was teaching me a lesson. I learned the lesson and accepted my culpability, never imagining it would lead to a ten-month separation.

I experienced isolation at church. I stepped down from ministry. I eventually had to leave that church.

Not only does doing the right thing not guarantee a positive outcome, sometimes doing the right thing just doesn't feel good. It would have felt much better to retaliate and get even. The Bible talks about the war that goes on between our flesh and the Spirit. There were times when I wanted to respond differently— out of my flesh.

Affirmation

God created both men and women with the need for affirmation, yet I believe men have a special need for affirmation that we do not always admit. A husband who is affirmed by his wife is a strong man. I can still recall with fondness the feelings I experienced at times when my wife affirmed me as a man. I felt that my struggles and sacrifices were worthwhile. I felt I was accomplishing what God wanted me to do in the lives of the ones He entrusted to me. I was encouraged to go on. I saved all the cards my wife would give me on special occasions because the encouraging words meant so much. She would take the time to pick out the card that expressed just what she felt, or either write the card herself. Those words were fuel for my emotional engine, even though "words of affirmation" is not my primary love language.

> *Even when a person is doing what he or she is supposed to do, it is still nice to hear words of appreciation.*

Even when a person is doing what he or she is supposed to do, it is still nice to hear words of appreciation. It lets the person know that his or her actions are not taken for granted. A responsibility can become a pleasure when a man knows he is valued for it.

Feeling unappreciated can cause many responses, including:

- •Lack of desire to do things for others anymore
- •Resentment
- •Gravitation toward people that make you feel appreciated. If that person is not your spouse, that can be a problem

Referring back to our parable of the prodigal son, we can see that what the older son really sought from his father was affirmation. This is a common need/desire among men. For many of us the desire is greater. Our own unique personalities, and our upbringing have an impact on this need.

We know that this parable is really mainly about the loving father, who represents our loving heavenly Father. It is clear by the father's response to his younger son, that he is a compassionate father, who is in touch with the needs of his children. That being the case, it is not a stretch to surmise that this father was aware of his oldest son's need for affirmation. After all, he knew the needs of his younger son. There was a more important lesson this son had to learn.

4

It's Up to You

It was my first Father's Day and a few days after our first wedding anniversary. Some of the events of that day are a blur. Others will be etched in my memory for the rest of my life.

My wife, daughter and I went to church that Sunday as we always did. After church we planned to drive the 30 miles to visit my parents. It was my dad's first father's day as a grandfather. We planned to go out to dinner. Before leaving for my parents', my wife and I got into an argument. If I recall correctly, it was over the father's day gift she had bought me, but I'm not sure. In my mind, I couldn't understand why she would want to mess up my special day by starting an argument. Just a month prior, I had made sure her first mother's day was a special and memorable event.

In our short marriage, we seemed to have issues on holidays, and I couldn't understand why. In my family growing up, holidays were always positive times. I looked forward to them. I was determined not to let my wife spoil another special day for me—

especially my first father's day. I told her so. I gathered our four-month old daughter, and the diaper bag, and went to my dad's without my wife.

My parents were obviously shocked to see the two of us arrive without my wife. I just stated that she didn't come with us, and we went on. They didn't ask any questions. We had a wonderful day. We went to dinner and spent the rest of the day at their house enjoying family time. The only thing that could have been better was having my wife with me. Sadly, I had gotten used to disappointment with her.

> *The only thing that could have been better was having my wife with me. Sadly, I had gotten used to disappointment with her.*

My daughter and I arrived back home late that night. My wife was sitting in the bed reading a book. My daughter was already asleep in the car, so I put her to bed. It seemed to me that my wife was waiting on me to get home so she could pick a fight. I believed she was embarrassed that my parents saw that she did not support her husband on his first father's day. This was the same husband who cared for her while she was sick for seven of the months of her pregnancy. The one who took a month off from work without pay to care for her and our newborn baby. The least she could do was celebrate my first father's day with me. Despite her issues with me as a husband, she could surely say I was a good father.

My wife had talked about leaving me several times before, which was quite disturbing to me. Before marriage we had vowed that divorce was not an option. We had only been married a year. I felt she wasn't giving the marriage a chance. Deep down, I really didn't believe she would leave, but was just expressing her frustration.

As the conversation that father's day night began to head in the familiar direction of her leaving, I decided to call her bluff. In doing so, I uttered words that I will have to live with for the rest of my life. I said to my wife, "You can leave, but you won't see our daughter again." In no way did I mean she wouldn't see our daughter again, but that's what I said. What I really meant was that if she did leave, I would fight for custody of our daughter. I was trying to get her to see what leaving could cost her. It wouldn't be just an easy thing to do. Still I thought that none of this would be a reality anyway. I thought my wife knew me well enough to know what I was doing. (I believe she did, but just took advantage of an opportunity to make her move.) She later told me that she believed my statement because I said it so calmly. "You weren't yelling," she said, "like in the heat of an argument."

After making my fateful statement, I took my wife by the arm to escort her to the door. I knew she would resist, and she did so. "You said you wanted to leave, so why are you fight-ing?" I asked. Again, I knew in my mind that I was not going to put my wife out, and I think she knew it too. I was calling her bluff. The reality was I had to go to work the next morning. I couldn't stay home with our daughter or get a babysitter. We didn't even have a babysitter at the time. Our daughter was four months old, and my wife was then a stay-at-home mom.

She resisted all the way to the door, then she pulled away from me. As she did, she fell down the carpeted steps to our basement. We got tangled up and I began to fall as well, but I was able to catch my balance on the handrail.

As I watched my wife reach the bottom of the stairs, my first and natural instinct was to go comfort her. In those few seconds of time that seemed like minutes, I struggled with myself about what to do. I got to the bottom of the stairs and could see that she wasn't hurt. Should I console her? Should I continue? If so she is going to get away with not being accountable for her words. I would again look like a pushover. I made the decision not to console her. That was a costly decision.

The episode ended, and I went to bed. My wife went to another room. After all that happened, I could not sleep. I lay in bed for hours thinking. At around 3 am, I heard my wife rustling around in the other room, then I heard the outside door open.

A few minutes later, I got up and went to the door to discover that my wife had left with our daughter. I didn't think this was that big of a deal.

A few minutes later, I got up and went to the door to discover that my wife had left with our daughter. I didn't think this was that big of a deal. The thing that bothered me was that she left the outside door wide open at 3:00 in the morning. I later learned that she thought I was asleep and waited for an opportunity to sneak out of the house. I felt she could have taken the extra two seconds to close the door so as not to leave the house vulnerable to thieves, since she thought I was asleep.

I went back to bed, and finally fell asleep. It was a hot night in June, so our windows were open. I was awakened later that morning by the sound of a radio dispatch operator outside of my bedroom window. It was not that unusual to hear a radio

---

dispatcher because one of our neighbors worked for the city. Some mornings one of the city trucks would be parked out front, and the dispatcher could be heard.

Soon afterwards, there was a knock on my front door. I got out of bed and went to the door. Standing on the porch was a police officer. I saw his partner walking around toward the back of the house like they do on police shows when they are going after a fugitive. I opened the door. "Are you Rodney Winters?" he asked. I told him yes. "I understand that there was a domestic disturbance here last night," he continued. "Your wife says that you caused her some injuries." I explained that she fell down the stairs. He explained to me that all it takes for there to be a charge of domestic violence is a perceived threat by the victim. He quoted a statement I had made the previous night that I acknowledged could have been perceived as a threat if a person wanted it to. The officer then informed me that he was placing me under arrest.

By this time, his partner had come in the door. They told me to put some clothes on, and they watched me as I went back to my bedroom and put on the first thing I could find. They handcuffed me and escorted me to their police cruiser.

> *The guy who only had one speeding ticket in his life and "never did anything wrong", was now on his way downtown.*

I remember thinking to myself, "She got me this time." I'm always the one holding other people accountable for their words and actions, so I didn't have a problem dealing with my consequences. Aside from the embarrassment, I was ok with the situation. Although I couldn't see them, I was sure some of my neighbors were looking out their windows seeing me arrested. Some neighbors went to the same church as my wife and I, and all of them knew I went to church. The guy who only had one speeding ticket in his life and "never did anything wrong", was now on his way downtown.

The worse thing about the timing of this event was that I had a deadline at work that day. I had to turn in a draft of a presentation I was giving for my management later that month. At this particular job, it was rare for me to have deadlines, so this was important. Of all days, it had to be this day. I did not miss deadlines or miss work.

I expected to be home later that day and everything to be back to normal. I envisioned my wife and I having a good discussion about the previous day, with me admitting I was wrong. With me being arrested, my wife would always have the upper hand. I could live with that. Those were my consequences.

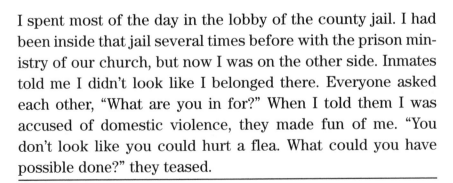

With me being arrested, my wife would always have the upper hand. I could live with that. Those were my consequences.

I spent most of the day in the lobby of the county jail. I had been inside that jail several times before with the prison ministry of our church, but now I was on the other side. Inmates told me I didn't look like I belonged there. Everyone asked each other, "What are you in for?" When I told them I was accused of domestic violence, they made fun of me. "You don't look like you could hurt a flea. What could you have possible done?" they teased.

Based on the shows I had seen on television, I expected to be allowed one phone call. There was a pay phone in the lobby, and I could make all the phone calls I wanted. I was there with another person the police had picked up on our way downtown. We sat and watched TV. They offered us breakfast, but I wasn't very hungry.

My job was in another city, and a long-distance phone call. I needed to report off from work. My friends and family were either a long-distance call also, or they were already at work, and I did not have their work numbers. This was before the time everyone had cell phones. I called my wife and asked her to call my job and report me off. I didn't see this as a problem. As I stated, I viewed this incident totally differently. I later learned that my wife was livid that I had the audacity to call her and ask her to call my job "after all I had done to her."

I also needed to get an attorney. The only attorney I or my family knew was a corporate attorney. No one I knew ever needed a criminal attorney. I finally was able to make some collect calls and retain the one corporate attorney I knew. The message got back to me that I would be out before the day was over.

That evening when I got out, things did not turn out like I expected. I learned that my wife was pressing charges against me, and had filed a restraining order against me. I never saw the restraining order, but I was told it stated I was a threat to my wife and our infant daughter. The part about my daughter really hurt me. Even if my wife believed I would hurt her, she knew for sure that I would never harm our daughter.

I was not allowed to return home, and was advised to not have any contact with my wife. I had to get a police escort to my house that night to retrieve my car and some clothes for work the next day. A friend of mine graciously allowed me to stay with him for a week or so. When I realized that this situation was going to drag on, I could not impose on him any longer, so I stayed with my parents.

The provisions of the restraining order only allowed me to see my daughter under the supervision of my parents. This was a hardship emotionally and logistically, as my parents lived 30 miles away. However, I struggled through the difficulty in order to have quality time with my daughter.

Finally, some time in August, my wife moved out and I was able to return home. She had gotten an apartment in another part of the city. Coming home was bittersweet because my wife and daughter were not there. Still, I had minimal contact with my wife.

I maintained financial responsibility for both residences. My wife had access to all of the finances, and proceeded to drain our bank accounts and charge large amounts on my credit cards.

> *I was willing to take that chance to stand up for what was right. My sense of right and wrong compelled me to do so.*

As the trial date approached, I was determined to fight the charges against me. There was no way I was going to accept the false accusations made against me. I was facing a maximum of a year in jail if I was convicted on the misdemeanor domestic violence charge. I was willing to take that chance to stand up for what was right. My sense of right and wrong compelled me to do so. Everyone around me—my family, my attorney, my counseling pastor—felt I should accept the plea bargain that was offered me. With the plea bargain, I would admit guilt and avoid any possible jail time. My advisors presented all kinds of arguments as to why the plea bargain would be best. However, I was not convinced. I had faith that God would vindicate me, and I believed in the justice system.

> *However, I was not convinced. I had faith that God would vindicate me, and I believed in the justice system.*

The prosecutor portrayed me as being the stereotypical abusive husband. My wife played the role of "the victim" to a tee. I believe she knew that I never have and never would hit her. She had used that fact to her advantage in the past. Now she was playing semantic games to say that a man should never put his hands on a woman. I had done so by grabbing her arm to escort her out of the house on father's day. Every time I hugged or caressed my wife I was putting my hands on her, but the police were never called for that.

The fact of the matter is, on two different occasions prior to this incident, my wife actually hit me during a disagreement. On neither occasion did I hit her back. I simply restrained her and got her under control. I would never call the police and say, "My wife hit me." I don't know any man who would. One of the times my wife actually broke my glasses when she hit me in the face.

If anyone should have been arrested for domestic violence, it should have been her. Years later she admitted to our pastor that I had never hit her, although she had hit me. I have yet to personally hear this admission. Again, I was feeling like the older brother of the prodigal son.

On the deadline date to accept the plea bargain, I finally agreed to it. After much prayer and counseling, I pleaded guilty to a misdemeanor domestic violence charge. My counseling pastor convinced me that the only chance I had of salvaging my marriage would be to plead guilty. He and others convinced me that I had too much to lose if I took the risk of a trial. I was an engineer with a master's degree in business. The risk was too great for me to go to jail and lose my career opportunities, etc. The judge and/or jury would be sympathetic to my wife. I did admit my culpability for the events that happened that father's day, and accepted my consequences.

My record has cost me a couple of employment opportunities to date. Also, people have a hard time believing a person would accept responsibility for something they didn't do. I was ostracized by my church family, and I was asked to step down from ministry.

Part of the stipulations were that I had to attend counseling. This was not a problem for me. I saw counseling as a benefit.

Ultimately, my wife and I got back together after ten months of separation, and I agree this would not have been possible if I had fought her in court.

> *But if we can step back for a moment and look beyond our circumstances to our loving heavenly Father, we can rest in the fact that He knows what is best for us.*

How should a man respond when life seems unfair? We can easily become cynical. The temptation can be great to give up. It can be easy to say, "what's the use?" We can look at others and falsely conclude that it doesn't pay to do right. But if we can step back for a moment and look beyond our circumstances to our loving heavenly Father, we can rest in the fact that He knows what is best for us.

The Bible does not tell us if this older son ever went into the house to join the celebration after his father's explanation. However, we can be sure that the father went back inside. He planned this great party, and he wasn't going to stay outside and miss the celebration. The guest of honor was inside. The loving father came out to meet both of his sons, but when he returned to the house, Junior had a decision to make. If he now wanted to experience the presence of his father, he had to go where his father was. We have a choice to make when in a similar situation. We can come into the presence of our loving heavenly Father and experience the joy that He gives us there, or we can remain outside and wallow in self-pity. We can choose to join the festivities or remain isolated. God has given us free will, and He does not force us to do anything. It's up to us. It's hard to sing and be angry at the same time. It's difficult to dance with our lip poked out. There's something about a party atmosphere that is contagious. We tell ourselves we're not going to move, but when the music starts playing, we find our foot tapping to the beat. Before we know it, we've forgotten about our problems for the moment.

We must choose to, "go into the house." The house represents the place where God, our Father, is. The house is a place of shelter. Just like as a child I found shelter from the rain in my parents' house, I can find shelter from the storms of life in the presence of God. The house is a place of comfort.

The bandage and medicine I needed for my scraped-up knee was located in the house. The balm and the soothing touch I need for my wounded heart or broken spirit are found in the presence of God.

The house is also a place of nourishment. When it was time to eat growing up, I would go into the house to eat my dinner. Likewise, when my hungry soul needs to be fed, there is a feast spread before me in the presence of God. The house is a place of rest. In the same way I went into the house when it was bedtime as a child, I can go into the presence of God to experience rest from the cares of this life. And sometimes the house is a place of celebration. It's where we go to have a party.

> *You may be asking, "How do I enter the Father's presence?" The answer is—in worship.*

You may be asking, "How do I enter the Father's presence?" The answer is—in worship. David said in Psalm 100, "Enter His gates with thanksgiving, and His courts with praise." Life may be difficult right now. You may not understand why things turned out the way they did, but you've got to learn to say, "Hallelujah," in spite of the circumstances. God is still worthy to be praised! Through our worship, we draw closer to God. He, in turn, draws closer to us as well.

Worship is a joyous experience, much like a party atmosphere. We celebrate who God is, and what He has done. When we enter the Father's presence, we also enjoy the Father's provision. Junior could come inside and eat, and be full. The resources were certainly available. There was the potential that this son could enjoy the same blessings as his younger brother. There were more calves where that one came from. His little brother may have received a ring, a robe, and some sandals, but those were not the only ones their father owned. No doubt this son was tired after a long, hard day in the field. Inside the house, he could find rest and be served. Not only that, the father assured his first-born son with the statement that "all that is mine is yours." Everything that the Father has, we have access to. Psalm 16:11 tells us that in His presence is fullness of joy, and at His right hand there are pleasures evermore. Matthew tells us that we also find rest in His presence. (11:28,29)

5

Standing for the Truth

As a man and leader of your household, you will be called upon to stand for the truth. When you do so, that opens you up to be attacked by Satan. Satan opposes the truth in every way. When you stand, you are a stationary target. However, you can stand wearing the full armor of God—the belt of truth, the breastplate of righteousness, the shoes of the preparation of the gospel of peace, the shield of faith, the helmet of salvation, and the sword of the Spirit. It is spiritual warfare, but you can win!

As a husband, you represent Christ and His relationship to the Church. That fact alone places the husband as a target for spiritual attack. Our command as husbands to love our wives as Christ loves the Church is an awesome challenge. Our example is our perfect Savior. How can we measure up? Jesus demonstrated His love by giving. His ultimate gift was His life. The opposite of love is not hate, but selfishness. If we are focused on ourselves, we are not expressing love—and vice versa.

Being a godly man means standing for the truth. In a world where there is increasingly no absolute truth, this is difficult to accomplish. Anyone who stands for the truth will be attacked. He will be labeled intolerant.

I have a strong value for the truth. Standing for the truth has cost me greatly throughout my life. I learned early on that people generally do not want to hear the truth. This can be seen even in our everyday conversations. When we ask a person how he or she is doing, we often really don't want to know. The question is often just a greeting. Our response to the question, "How are you?" is often untrue. We could be having the worse day of our lives, and our response is the usual, "Fine" or "I'm okay". We're not okay! The truthful answer is, "I'm deeply depressed. I feel like strangling someone right now. Or, I'm greatly disappointed." I observed that people lie so easily, even when it seems unnecessary. People would rather "be nice" than tell the truth. Admittedly, I was one who spoke the truth, but not always in love. God has been working on me to temper my tongue, and to be more compassionate. Even when love was present, I found that the truth was still not often well-received.

> *For management, telling the customer the truth meant the company would look bad or sometimes be at fault. That perception had to be avoided at all costs.*

In the workplace, standing for the truth limited my advancement. For management, telling the customer the truth meant the company would look bad or sometimes be at fault. That perception had to be avoided at all costs. I sat in many meetings in which the discussion was to figure out what to tell the customer. The whole truth was seldom an option. The group would decide on what spin to put on the real facts, and how to present them. I was uncomfortable with this.

> *I mentioned earlier that our premarital counselor cautioned my wife and I about our negative assumptions about each other.*

I mentioned earlier that our premarital counselor cautioned my wife and I about our negative assumptions about each other. The negative assumption I had about my wife was that she was a liar. She would often say things that simply were not true. I had a lot of difficulty with this, and we worked through a lot of it in counseling. I had to learn that my wife processed her emotions through talking. In other words, she would think out loud. Everything she would say would not be congruent because she was working through her thoughts as she spoke. I, on the other hand, process my emotions internally. When I speak, I have usually already thought through in my mind the different scenarios. What comes out is the conclusion of those thoughts. Our differences in communication styles caused problems in our marriage.

Although I tried not to let my negative assumption turn into a belief, events in our marriage kept leading me toward that conclusion. I would be confused because my wife would say things that didn't line up with things she had stated previously. I wanted to believe her, but I didn't know what to believe sometimes. My view of her was that when she was in a tough situation, she would say whatever she had to say to get out of it. She had a way of using words to her advantage. The problem for her was that I was her match when it came to that. She admitted that all of her life she had been able to get away with it, but she couldn't do so with me.

There were times when the apparent lies could be traced to definitional differences we had. For example, one time we had some friends over and we were discussing the little nagging habits that couples deal with, like which way to roll the toilet paper or squeezing the toothpaste at the wrong end. One of our guests mentioned the pet peeve of having his wife's underwear hanging in the bathroom. This was an issue for me because my wife did this. We had two bathrooms, but at the time, the one we were using the most was the one that guests would use when they came over. If my friends came by unexpectedly, I would have to make sure my wife hadn't left her underwear hanging in the bathroom for guests to see.

When my friend mentioned this particular habit, my wife responded that she did not do this. I was in disbelief that she would say what I concluded to be an outright lie. We discussed it later, after everyone had gone. To my wife, the term "underwear" only refers to panties, briefs, underpants, etc. A bra would not be included in this definition. To me, "underwear" included all of the above. It was true that my wife did not leave her panties hanging in the bathroom—only her bras. Based on her definition, she was not lying. I had to learn these differences.

On the other hand, there were unquestionable lies. Promises made to me would not be kept, and there was always an excuse to justify the broken promises. My wife began to feel she couldn't talk to me because she felt her words were being analyzed, and would be used against her in the future. My goal was understanding, so if a statement she made was different from what she said previously, I would ask for clarification. My plan was to spend the rest of my life with this woman, so I desired to understand everything about her—including her thought processes. She just wanted to be heard, not questioned.

Because I value the truth, it is especially painful for me when lies are told about me. I have done enough wrong in my life that I have to deal with, without being accused of things that I did not do. People seemed eager to hear the lies. I guess it made them feel better about their shortcomings. My wife had a way of putting a spin on events that made them totally different than the way I perceived them. It was as if we were describing two totally different events.

> *Satan does not play by the rules. It seemed he used every weapon he could in my case. I had to constantly appropriate the armor of God in my life.*

Our role as a man is often one of a warrior. I was called upon to engage in intense spiritual warfare against the powers of darkness that had attacked my family and me personally. It was not a fair fight. Satan does not play by the rules. It seemed he used every weapon he could in my case. I had to constantly appropriate the armor of God in my life. The temptation was sometimes strong for me to respond in like fashion, but I had to resist. I had to trust that God would eventually work things out. I didn't always succeed in resisting.

Throughout the pain of my divorce process and in the aftermath of the adultery, I just had a longing for what was right. Daily, things were happening that were just wrong; were just evil. I did not desire for the guilty parties to be punished, I just wanted what was right. Even in terms of the outcomes, I just wanted what was right. If, from that day forward, my wife would have repented and committed to the marriage, none of the past would have mattered to me. I pleaded to God that righteousness would prevail. I knew that it ultimately would, but I desperately desired to see it at that moment. It was difficult to watch someone continue to do wrong with no ramifications. I prayed that the people involved in the wrongdoing would repent. Sadly, there was never even any acknowledgement of wrongdoing.

> *I pleaded to God that righteousness would prevail. I knew that it ultimately would, but I desperately desired to see it at that moment.*

Even the police refused to enforce the court order that prohibited my wife from removing items from our house during the divorce process. The officers stood and watched as my wife loaded her car with many of our household items. One of them even said I was being petty for wanting to abide by the court ruling. He said to me, "By your standards I should give a ticket to a driver who goes 41 MPH in a 40 MPH zone."

The insurance company that I had for the previous thirteen years—even before I was married—allowed my estranged wife to add a new vehicle she purchased to our joint policy. This was also a violation of the court order. The mailing address for the bill was changed to a post office box my wife acquired. I did not have keys or access to the car or post office box, yet I was expected to pay for both. The insurance company rep stated that because we were still legally married, my wife could get away with it.

In most cases, it has been my experience that the man sets the tone for the course of his family. Generally, if there is a godly man leading a household, the family will follow. Far too often we hear of women who desire to live godly and pursue righteousness, but they are married to men who are not strong godly leaders. That man can bring a curse on his family. But usually when the husband is following the Lord, the family follows. I asked God why I had to be an exception to the rule. Even with my mistakes, my heart was for God and for my family. My wife may not have always agreed with the way I went about doing things, but I did what I believed was best for my family. Some decisions I made were bad ones, but we have to move on. I was portrayed as an evil person, which I was not.

Still as a man, and head of my household, I had little or no control over the outcome of my marriage at a certain point. I did not believe it was too late to reconcile, or that there had been too much damage done. Nonetheless, nothing I could do would change the situation in my home. There was a deep sense of helplessness. Prayer was my only tool.

There was a deep sense of helplessness. Prayer was my only tool.

Demonic attack came in the area of truth. Satan is the father of lies. Lies were being told to me on a regular basis. At the same time, lies were being told about me to others. As is typical with Satan, there was always some truth in the statements that were made. This made the lie easier to believe. It was classic deception. So many acts were being done in secret—spending money, telephone calls, sneaking out of the house. Secrecy became the norm in our household. My role became to expose and to shine light. God has given me a great deal of discernment. I am often easily able to tell the truth from a lie. I am analytical by nature and also by education and training as an engineer. I am very observant of people's nonverbal communication cues such as body language. I make note of eye contact and fidgeting.

> *Secrecy became the norm in our household. My role became to expose and to shine light.*

The lying was an insult to me. It was an indication to me of my wife's view of me. I believed if there was anybody one could be totally honest with, it would be ones spouse. Home was supposed to be the place where you could be yourself, and be accepted. It was obvious she thought I didn't know she wasn't telling the truth. After a while, I did not let on that I knew I was being lied to. Or if I did, I didn't reveal my proof. I believe this gave my wife a false sense of confidence that she could continue to lie to me and get away with it. The lies seemed to increase. Sometimes I just wanted to see how far she would go with her story.

My wife told me her view was that if you love someone, you don't tell him or her negative things like, "You've gained weight." I, on the other hand, wanted my wife to be honest with me, whether it was positive or negative. I wanted her to tell me things that bothered her about me, so that I could work on them. She rarely did except for during heated arguments.

Then the issue would often be blown out of proportion and become a personal attack.

My wife even lied under oath to the magistrate during our divorce hearings. I naively believed there would be repercussions for perjury, but the magistrate did not care.

Ironically, when I was pleading with my wife to consider reconciliation, her response to me was that she did not want to be married to someone who viewed her as a liar and an adulterer. She made the issue to be how I viewed her, rather than dealing with the truth of those two facts. Loving her as Christ loves the church required me to hold her accountable, though not viewing her as a sinner.

> *The book of Proverbs is full of statements of what will be the fate of an evil person based on his deeds, but how do these statements apply to a Christian?*

How does a man respond when evil is being perpetrated against him by another believer? This question forced me to reconsider my view of heaven. The book of Proverbs is full of statements of what will be the fate of an evil person based on his deeds, but how do these statements apply to a Christian?

These were believers as well, so their sins have been paid for on the cross. I didn't view myself as naïve. I saw myself as just the opposite. But the more sin that was exposed, the more I had to reconsider my self-perception. Maybe I wasn't as wise as I thought I was. Maybe my expectations of Believers were too great. These were professing Christians in high leadership positions in the church, with effective ministries, by all appearances.

I felt like Elijah did after confronting the prophets of Baal on Mt. Carmel. He thought he was the only one left who was serving God. God had to let him know that there were many others who were committed to Him. I asked, where was the conviction of the Holy Spirit in these people's lives? A true Believer should be penitent.

I struggled with this. Some people who observed the situation questioned the salvation of those involved in the sinful behaviors. If nothing else they were at the point of self-deception and possibly a seared conscience. I was also surprised and disappointed by the amount of support received for sinful behavior by other professing Christians. My wife had friends who knew about and supported her adulterous relationship. They were even involved in covering for her when she would lie about her whereabouts.

I knew that I was to forgive my brother or sister in Christ, but my question had to do with God's response to His sinful child. How could a person continue in sin and seemingly have no consequences? I believe God's word that He disciplines His children whom He loves, but I often do not see it. One believer is trying to live right and another is blatantly sinning. Both will ultimately end up in heaven. The one will suffer loss of reward, but what does that really mean? Since we know there will be no envy or jealousy in heaven, what difference will it make that I have four crowns and you have two? Those who have been faithful over a few things on earth will be ruler over many in the kingdom of heaven. In heaven, do I have to look forward to serving those I have mistreated in this life? Obviously, heaven will not be the way we often picture it in our minds. We often think about just making it to heaven and avoiding the torment of hell, but there must be more to it than that.

Contrary to what people frequently say, there will be tears in heaven. The Bible says that God will wipe away all tears from their eyes. (Revelation 7:17, 21:4) The tears have to be present in order to be wiped away. At the Judgment Seat of Christ, there will be weeping and gnashing of teeth. All believers must give an account of what we have done in this life with what God has entrusted to us. We are told that those who have been unfaithful will suffer loss. I believe there will be tears of regret.

The challenge is to live is such a manner that I will receive the greatest reward possible. I, for one, don't want to be empty-handed when the saints cast their crowns before God's throne.

The Bible says that the sufferings of this life are not worthy to be compared to the glory that shall be revealed in us. (Romans 8:18) Does this mean that we will just forget about the trials we have endured down here when we experience the glorious splendor of the presence of God? Will we even care about being vindicated at that point? Will others see and know? I can imagine people apologizing to me after learning the truth, but I'm not sure this is a realistic view of the events in heaven.

I don't have the answers to these questions. I began to see more of God's patient and forgiving nature. I seemed to usually have to face the consequences for my actions. Where was my crop failure? This is where engaging the Father in prayer came into play. I eventually had to release these people to the Lord. They were His responsibility.

6

Letting Go

Christmas Eve (continued)

> *"Let me cover you with kisses and discover new*
> *ways to make you happy.*
> *Let me touch you deep, until every part of me is*
> *one with every part of you.*
> *Let me love you like you deserve to be loved."*

These are the words on the card I found on Christmas Eve. They expressed the sentiments of *my* wife to another man. Quickly all the signs I had seen before became clear. There was still a level of denial within me. I rationalized that perhaps my wife intended to give me that card, but changed her mind at the last minute. In spite of not receiving that card, I wanted to spend the day as a family, so I thought the kids and I would go with my wife to a nearby city and just be with her at her booth. (She had told me the night before about a bazaar that was occurring on Christmas day at a hospital, that she was going to attend to sell her Avon products.)

I didn't think this would be a problem. I had planned to tell her of my intensions, but the time just got away. She spent several hours, if not the whole morning, talking on the phone with her family. When my wife got off the phone, I made my calls to my family. When I got off the phone, she was almost ready to go. The time had gotten away. I told her that the kids and I were going with her to XYZ. She became agitated. She was ready to leave and I asked if she would wait for us. She said no because she had to pick up another woman and they had to go to the Avon store to pick up product. She said she was supposed to be there at 2:00, and it was already 2:00. She said that we could meet her there. I asked which hospital she was going to, but she wouldn't tell me. She said, "You used to work in XYZ, so you should know about the hospital." I commented that there was more than one hospital in XYZ. Still she refused to tell me. After I pressed her for an answer, she said she didn't know—that her passenger had all the information. She told me to look on the internet. She stated that the kids would need something to eat first, and then she left. I noticed that she didn't take any of her Avon products, books, etc. She was wearing an outfit that didn't seem appropriate for selling Avon.

I was encouraged by the fact that my wife told me we could meet her there, even though other things didn't add up. I concluded that the event must be real, but maybe she hadn't planned on going, or at least staying until 9:00 p.m., as she told me. I figured she would at least make an appearance since we were meeting her there.

I got the kids some food, got them ready and set off for XYZ. We left after 3:00. It had now begun to snow. We went to the main hospital in that city and asked about the event, but no one knew anything about it. They asked if I was sure it was at that particular hospital, and I said no. Before I left home, I had gotten the passenger's cell phone number from my wife's Avon book, which she didn't take with her. I called the passenger's cell phone, since she was supposedly the one who had the information. There was no answer. I found that strange since she was an Avon manager who uses her cell phone for business, and was on the road or at a sales function.

However, that would make sense if this woman was spending Christmas with her family like most people. I called my wife's cell phone and told her we were at the hospital, and asked her what hospital she was at. She said they were still in our city at the Avon store and hadn't even left yet. It was now around 4:30. She said she had to ask her rider which hospital. She went away from her phone, then came back and gave me a different hospital name. The way she did that set off a red flag in my mind. Since she was on a cell phone, she could have walked over to the person and asked the question in my hearing. She said they were on their way and would meet us at the second hospital in 40 minutes.

I was suspicious, but still believed she would at least meet us there, although I knew it would take longer than 40 minutes from our town. I didn't believe my wife would send me on a wild goose chase knowing I had the kids with me, and how bad the weather had gotten that day. I got directions to the second hospital and headed there. By this time it was about 4:45.

The guy at the second hospital said, "It's Christmas, we don't have that sort of thing on Christmas." That was as I had suspected. Still I expected my wife to show up with one of her classic excuses, since she promised to meet us. I decided to give her until 6:00, a reasonable time to get there from our city. I didn't have a cell phone at this time. After 6:00, I called her again since she hadn't shown up. She said she was on her way back home, and that she tried calling me at the first number I called from but there was no answer. (I believe she knew that was the hospital pay phone.) She said, "Anything you have to say, we can discuss when you get home." I was confused and in disbelief. I said, "What are you talking about? I thought you were meeting us at this Avon benefit?" She replied, "Whatever," and ended the call.

> *As we were sliding, I was just thinking about the safety of the kids. The impact was such that I expected the airbag to deploy, but it didn't.*

I buckled the kids in the car and headed home. The drive home was a blur. The kids were confused. I was confused. I was hurt, disappointed, frustrated, shocked. The roads were terrible due to the ice and snow, and the drive was slow. I never got above 45 MPH in a 65 MPH zone. I was not looking forward to what I would have to face when I got home. The hour-long drive turned into more like an hour and a half. We just got into the city limits when I started to swerve on a patch of ice. I tried to avoid hitting a minivan that was on my right and lost control of the car. We slammed into the concrete median wall on the freeway. As we were sliding, I was just thinking about the safety of the kids. The impact was such that I expected the airbag to deploy, but it didn't.

After impact I immediately looked in the back seat to see if the children were okay. They were fine. I thanked the Lord.

As we sat there facing the oncoming traffic, unable to move, I began to lament the senselessness of that accident, and the potentially serious outcome. Also, I had just gotten that car three days prior, now the front end was all banged up. I entertained the possibility of this being my fault for getting on the road in the first place. I recognized that my motives were pure in that I legitimately wanted the family to be together on Christmas, even if it meant us sitting with my wife at a sales booth. I had to conclude that if my wife hadn't lied, we wouldn't be in that situation. Even if she had come clean when we were at the first hospital, the hour and a half earlier we would have left XYZ probably would have allowed us to avoid the accident. The roads were cleaner then, and it wasn't yet dark. I wondered to myself if my wife would regret lying to me when she realized we could have been killed. I thought that might be a wakeup call for her.

When we got home the kids immediately told my wife that "we crashed", and I gave her more details. She didn't seem very concerned, but she did go to the garage and take a look at the car. She didn't mention anything about talking, and I wasn't in the mood. In addition, the kids were still awake. I went into the bedroom, sat in the dark and prayed for a while. Then I decided I needed to talk to someone else, so I drove to a payphone so my wife couldn't hear my conversation. As a talked, I figured by the time I got home my wife would be in the bed, and we wouldn't be able to talk. That turned out to be the case. I figured we would have to wait until the following night after the kids went to bed. I naively assumed that since it was obvious that I had caught her in a series of lies, she would admit it and tell me the truth.

Circumstances occurred such that the next morning I was up while my wife was getting ready for work. I asked her what the previous night was all about. She said it was about her not playing my games while I tried to be Sherlock Holmes and follow her around. That wasn't the response I expected. From my view, I was not following her around. I reminded her that she was the one who told us to meet her in XYZ. I wanted us to ride together. She said I waited until the last minute to say something when I had planned all along to check up on her. I reminded her that she didn't tell me about the event until about 11 pm the night before. She said, "You're a planner, and you knew all along what you were going to do. I wasn't going to play a part in your games." I told her how the time got away from me on Christmas and that I just wanted the family to spend time together.

> *It didn't make sense to me for a person to get something they say they've wanted for a long time, then reject it.*

She made the statement that I never wanted to spend time with the family any other time. That was an absurd statement, yet she had made it several times before. She questioned why all of a sudden I wanted to spend time with the family. I told her how I was disappointed that we didn't spend Thanksgiving together and didn't want to do the same thing on Christmas. She stated that she always wants to do family things, but I never do. I disputed that, but asked even if that were true, why not be happy that I started yesterday, since you say that's what you want me to do? She answered, because she wasn't going to participate in my games. It didn't make sense to me for a person to get something they say they've wanted for a long time, then reject it.

As the conversation continued, I asked about the supposed benefit in XYZ. My wife said she actually thought there was a benefit, but that turned out not to be the case. She continued to lie to try to cover her previous lies. She said the real reason she left at 2:00 was to meet with her passenger to discuss her options regarding divorcing me. She said her passenger is an attorney. I couldn't verify that, but it was not consistent with what my wife told me in the past about her. I don't think she remembered that she had told me about this woman previously. She had told me previously this woman makes $100,000 a year selling Avon. There would be no need to practice law, and when would she have the time? My wife told me she had been trying to meet with this woman for three months, but she never had the time. Christmas was the only day she could squeeze my wife in. My wife said that if this woman had met with her at her office, she would have to bill her, but if she did it on her own time (i.e. Christmas) she would not have to bill her. That made no sense to me. If an attorney doesn't want to bill a person, they just don't bill them. It doesn't matter when or where they meet.

My wife restated that this woman was going to buy her inventory, and that she lives in XYZ. That statement I knew to be a lie. This woman lived in another city, but my wife didn't know that I knew that. My wife said because the woman lives in XYZ, she has a lot of clients at the hospital and they were going there to try to sell Avon. They were going to discuss the divorce on the way, but my wife believed there actually was a benefit. The story was not lining up. If the woman actually lived in XYZ, My wife would have had to drive to XYZ, pick her up, drive back to our city to the Avon store, then drive back to

XYZ to the hospital. Although I knew my wife was lying, I did not refute what she said. I just listened. I often do this, and I believe my wife thinks she is fooling me because I don't say anything. This has happened countless times. I asked if she was actually in XYZ that day and she said yes. That I believed. I asked my wife why she couldn't tell me the truth about where she was going since she has been so open and vocal in the past about wanting a divorce. Why was it such a secret now? I don't remember her exact answer, but I recall it sounding very lame to me.

My wife proceeded to reprimand me for taking the kids away from their toys on Christmas day to drive them around in the car with me. She said on Christmas, kids are supposed to spend the whole day playing with the toys they got. She said if she had known I was going to do that, she would have stayed at home. (Again, it was my fault for waiting until the last minute.) She said she had not been able to get together with this woman for three months, so if she had missed this opportunity it wouldn't have been a big deal. Earlier on Christmas, my wife asked me if I was taking the kids with me to visit my relatives in another nearby city. She was hoping I would, but I had no plans to. (That would give her clear passage to do her thing.) Now she was saying kids should be at home on Christmas.

I asked my wife point blank if she was having an affair. She avoided the question three times. She said something to the effect of, "What difference does it make; we don't have a relationship?" After the fourth time I asked, I guess she realized I was going to keep asking until she answered, and she finally said "no". Some time during the conversation my wife stated that it was all about me not trusting her.

My wife spent most of the rest of the conversation telling me about myself and how I was the reason for the terrible condition of our marriage. Most of it I'd heard before, but there were a few new interesting revelations. I basically listened and made a few comments here and there. She said I was making her late for work, yet she continued to do most of the talking. Finally she was late, the conversation ended, and she left for work. I was actually surprised she allowed herself to be late for work just to have that conversation with me. I guess she had a lot of anger she needed to get off her chest.

> *I couldn't believe how bold she was, knowing I would see the phone bill. Yet, she wouldn't tell me the truth.*

On New Year's day I opened some mail I had gotten earlier in the week but never opened. On my long distance bill were several calls to a number in the city we drove to on Christmas and one in the neighboring city to it. I could tell by the number that one was a cell phone. I knew instinctively that those calls were to my wife's boyfriend. Even after everything that happened, that still surprised me. I couldn't believe how bold she was, knowing I would see the phone bill. Yet, she wouldn't tell me the truth.

There were 12 calls on three days for a total of 182 minutes. That's over three hours. More than two of the hours were when I was away from home making arrangements to get the car I wrecked on Christmas. The second day was a call that lasted over an hour. The third day was a one-minute call, so he probably wasn't home. My wife hadn't talked to me for a total of three hours in the previous few months. That bill ended on December 21, so I suspected there would be more calls after that. The total was less than $30, but I planned to make her pay it.

Just to have proof, I went to a pay phone and I called the numbers. A man answered the home number, then a woman picked up another phone. I hung up and called the cell phone number. I got the voice mail, and it was the same man's voice. He identified himself as the person I suspected—my wife's former boss. The fact that a woman answered his home phone made me wonder if he had a wife or girlfriend himself. I later found out he lived with his mother!

> *The signs of my wife's unfaithfulness had been there, but I rationalized them away.*

A few weeks later, I found a credit card receipt from my wife that was dated on Christmas day. The time printed on it was a few minutes after she left the house. It was from one of the few stores that was open on Christmas. The receipt was for a fairly expensive electronic item. I never saw the item. We already had one of these items in our house, so it wasn't for us. I concluded that this was a Christmas gift for the person she was meeting that day—namely her boyfriend. This added further insult to the meager gift she bought me.

The signs of my wife's unfaithfulness had been there, but I rationalized them away. I told myself she wouldn't be doing such a thing at this stage of our marriage. Though things had been bad in the past, I had seen an improvement. We talked more. We didn't argue like we used to. I felt we were beginning to understand one another better. Now we had two children, which implied we had different priorities. We recently bought a new house and were trying to make a new beginning. My wife had recently become a minister in our church. From my perspective, she had accepted a call to a higher standard. Her actions were uncharacteristic of that calling.

This was not, however, my wife's first affair. She admitted to having an "emotional affair" with another man during our period of separation after two years of marriage. I had evidence to suggest it was more than emotional, but that was all she admitted to. She had always told me that if I ever had an emotional affair with another woman, it would be worse for her than if I had a physical, sexual affair. Because of my wife's past, sex was often meaningless to her. She knew I would never cheat on her sexually, but she stated to me that the idea of me being emotionally intimate with someone else, even though I did not have sex with her, would be far more devastating. I never forgot those conversations. Now at this point she was telling me she had an emotional affair as if it wasn't such a bad thing.

I listed the following indications I had noticed previously that suggested my wife was having an affair:

- I noticed her putting on makeup; getting her hair done frequently; buying and wearing new clothes.

- There was decreased interest in dealing with me without any apparent reason (no arguments). After we had a discussion, she used it to justify her actions.

- There was a return back to privacy and secrecy when it came to getting dressed/being naked in my presence. She had become more free in this area.

• It had not been uncommon for us to go months without sex, but this time was the longest we'd ever gone, and there was no apparent reason. When we would finally have intercourse, she would say it was because she knew I wanted it or she felt guilty about it being so long. I always believed it was because of her own needs. The long time period this time made me wonder if she was getting her needs met somewhere else.

• Our daughter asked her what was the man's name where she works (or used to work). My wife became visibly uncomfortable and after a pause responded, "His name is Mr. Manager." Before that she would openly mention his name. It was apparent to me that our daughter was telling on her.

• I noticed my wife leaving late for work and she didn't seem to care. She said she could leave/take lunch whenever she wanted. She was interviewing for another job during work hours. She said her boss knew she was looking for another job when she started, and he allowed her to do so.

• When my wife first started working at this job, she said she couldn't actively sell her Avon; she could only display her books. I later found out her boss allowed her to actively sell. It was apparent that she was getting special treatment from her boss.

• After quitting that job, she would often go back. She had a legitimate reason—to deliver Avon, but I was suspicious. She would lie about her reason, which indicated to me she was trying to cover up something.

• My wife told me that every Friday or Saturday evening she was going to go out with one of her two best friends.

- My wife started back on her diet pills.

- She told me she was going to be rejoining the YMCA. This was to get back to her exercise routine.

The more I began to investigate, the more things I began to uncover. I could not believe what I was discovering. At times it felt as if I was living in a bad dream. It seemed surreal. I kept telling myself, this cannot be happening. The blatancy of many of my wife's actions was difficult to reconcile in my mind. This was the woman who promised to love me until death. She was a believer in Christ, like myself. Where was the conviction of the Holy Spirit?

> *It was at those times that I could see how previous negative situations God had allowed in my life were working for my good.*

Strangely, some of the things that were done to me were a testament to my character. Despite all the things that were said to the contrary, my wife knew I would "do the right thing". I believe most women would have been afraid to do to their husbands the kind of things my wife did to me. She knew what she could get away with as it related to me. I had to learn the delicate balance of holding her accountable, and trusting God with the outcome. So often I wanted to react, but the Lord kept me from doing so. It was at those times that I could see how previous negative situations God had allowed in my life were working for my good. Had I not gone through those experiences, my response would have been very different—to my detriment. At the time I was going through those experiences, I could not see the purpose. There were very few people with whom I could even share what was really going on. My very manhood was being attacked. Most people would not understand my response. They would think I was being a wimp or a pushover. One could say I was enabling my wife. For me, I understood that none of her actions was worth me losing my freedom. I believe God allowed me to spend those few hours inside of the county jail to ensure that I wouldn't end up there permanently. He knew that a few years down the road I would be faced with situations that could cause me to explode in anger and make a stupid decision.

In spite of my belief about I Corinthians 10:13, there is a sense that God has allowed me to go through this level of trial because He knows I can handle it—though not on my own. God was teaching me some things.

I had to take one day at a time. I couldn't think too far into the future. I would be overwhelmed if I did. Court dates loomed overhead, and so many questions remained unanswered. My future was hanging in the balance. Where would I live? Which one of us would have primary custody of the kids? How much money would I have to pay?

I was inspired to write the lyrics and music to the following song. This was my prayer and heart's cry during my trial:

When the pain seems more than I can bear,
And I just can't find You anywhere.
Draw me unto You, Jesus.
Draw me unto You.

When my heart is drowning in despair,
I'm alone and no one seems to care.
Draw me unto You, Jesus.
Draw me unto You.

You made me a promise I can clearly see.
If I would draw near to You, You'd draw near to me.

When the path ahead is so unclear,
And the darkness causes me to fear.
Draw me unto You, Jesus.
Draw me unto You.

With Your lovingkindness, keep drawing me
'Til I'm in Your presence, and Your face I see.

When I've given all that I can give,
And I've almost lost my will to live.
Draw me unto You, Jesus.
Draw me unto You.

Draw me nearer, nearer blessed Lord
Draw me unto You, Jesus.
Draw me unto You.
Draw me unto You.
Draw me unto You.

© 2003 Rodney A. Winters

I had to ask myself (and God) the question if I was reaping the harvest of bad seeds I had previously sown. Although my life has been far from perfect, and I've made numerous mistakes, the answer came back no.

Recovering From Failure

The first step to recovering from failure is to admit that you have failed. Admitting failure is not easy—especially for men. We tend to make excuses or blame others. We must confess our sins to God and repent of the sins that have caused us to fall. King David was honest with God and with himself about his sin when he committed adultery and murder. (Psalm 51) I have had many successes in my life in many areas—academics, finance, career. I would trade them all for success in my marriage. Having a wife and family was something I desired and waited for for many years. I truly loved the wife and family that was given to me. I thought I was prepared to handle the challenge that was before me, but I came up short. I have come to understand that some of the failure was due to my efforts to handle things on my own, and not rely on God to do the work. This has been a hard lesson for me to learn. I failed to pray like I should have at times. I wasn't always sensitive to the nature of the spiritual warfare I was engaged in. I let my flesh get in the way too often. I ask myself those "what-if" questions.

> *I believe one of the keys to recovering from failure is experiencing forgiveness from those we have hurt.*

I believe one of the keys to recovering from failure is experiencing forgiveness from those we have hurt. Unfortunately this is not always possible. Those individuals we have offended may be unwilling to forgive. They may no longer be alive. One can still, however, experience God's forgiveness. It only requires repentance and confession on our part. (I John 1:9) I praise God that He has forgiven me from every sinful act I committed against my wife. He does not hold my past against me. I am not bound by feelings of guilt, but am free to move on.

A man must also be willing to be on the giving end of forgiveness. Colossians 3:13 says that we should forgive others just as we have been forgiven. We cannot afford to fall into the trap of bitterness. I heard a pastor say that the difference between bitter and better is "i". "I" have control over how I respond to the situations and people who have affected my life. I must make the choice to be better. I must choose to forgive. Extending forgiveness is not so much for the person who has wronged us, as it is for ourselves. Many times the person that we are holding hostage with our unforgiveness is not even aware or affected by it. We are the one who is being eaten up on the inside by our resentment. We lose sleep or experience other health issues, such as headaches or high blood pressure. We become agitated when we think about what that person has done to us. We need to release that person and trust God to make things right.

In spite of all the pain I have experienced, it has still been easy for me to forgive my wife for the things she has done. I recognize that she is not the enemy, but Satan. I still loved her deeply after the affairs, and I didn't foresee that changing. I understand that many of her actions are borne out of deep pain in her life. I believe there are some strongholds that still need to be torn down. I hurt for her because of the pain I know she has experienced. I also know that the enemy has blinded her to the truth in many areas. If she could have seen clearly, I know she would have responded differently. If she really knew the impact of some of her choices, I have to believe she would not have made some of them. I have seen glimpses of her true heart, and know that the person I am currently seeing is not the real person I married. My prayer is that her heart will be healed, and that it will be healed soon. I do not pray this for my sake, but for hers. I recognize that she is a child of God, and that He loves her just as much as He loves me. God's heart is grieved even more than mine because He sees everything. She is also still the mother of my children, and they need her to be whole... They need a godly example.

The difficult part for me was letting go. I had the faith to believe that all things were possible—even the restoration of my shattered marriage. At times I felt I was giving up on God as I let go. I wondered if I was stopping short, just before He was about the bless me. I could still see the great potential that existed with my wife and myself. I believe Satan saw it too, and tried to prevent it. I had to entrust my wife into God's hands, realizing He is even able to reunite a couple after a divorce.

I told myself that I would wear my wedding ring until the day my divorce was final. I had kept it on the entire ten months my wife had been separated several years previously. Removing my ring signaled a recognition that my marriage was over.

One of the things my wife and I told each other before we got married was that divorce was not an option. We even discussed the fact that an affair was not necessarily a reason to get a divorce. Yet, I found myself sitting with my attorney in front of a magistrate, across for my wife and her attorney. Someone who had only met us that morning would be determining very critical aspects of the future of our lives.

It was difficult to watch my hopes and dreams fade away before my eyes. I had to begin to grieve the loss and move forward to what God had for me. I did not want to move forward without my wife, but it was clear I had to. My heart ached for my two young children, who I knew would be negatively impacted by this for years to come. The impact on them could already be seen. I wanted to leave a positive legacy for them, not the sting of divorce. They didn't understand what was going on around them. They were too young to comprehend the complex scenario that was being played out before their eyes.

I had to learn that my love for my wife had to be manifested in a different way now. My role was changing. The pending divorce did not negate the vow I made on our wedding day. Loving now meant holding accountable.

I do not believe I "married the wrong person". I did not enter into that covenant haphazardly. Issues were there from the beginning, and were not a surprise to me. To a certain extent, I knew what I was getting into. One can look back and say that I should have known certain things would happen, or that I ignored the signs. The presence of these issues did not necessarily mean things would turn out the way they did. Other couples have overcome similar obstacles. There were a lot of personal choices involved. Small things were allowed to grow into not-so-small things. Many issues remained not dealt with. Unforgiveness played a major role also in the demise of the relationship.

> *Unforgiveness played a major role also in the demise of the relationship.*

Looking back, I did not have the same sense of urgency as my wife to have a better marriage, because I had a long-term perspective. The problems we were having didn't ultimately discourage me. Admittedly, they were frustrating, but I had hope and expectation that we would get through them. I expected to be married for the rest of my life. I knew the improvements would take time. We didn't get to our present state overnight. I could envision the day when things would be better between us. I often thought and sometimes said, "One day we're going to look back on these difficulties and realize how we've grown from them." At one point I did try to force things to get better, but I had to learn to wait on the proper timing. I didn't anticipate being divorced.

My wife seemed to look for any reason or justification for her decision to end the marriage. I could sense that she just wanted to be with this man she was seeing. If I didn't know who my wife was talking about, and heard the things she was saying about me to others, I would strongly dislike "this person" as well. She could be very convincing in her version of events. After she moved out, I found a list she had written for her attorney of all the negative things I had done throughout the marriage. The distortion of facts was painful to read. I know she truly believed her perceptions were fact.

There was a great sense of helplessness on my part. There was absolutely nothing I could do about certain things. I was completely powerless. I was totally dependent upon God. I had to learn that even when a person desires to do right, when he or she is in a relationship with another person, the other person may not have the same desire. Both parties must agree in order to have harmony.

> *There are choices that we make in the course of our lives that often determine where we end up.*

I never wanted to end up in the state of divorce. I suppose that is an obvious statement. No couple that gets married does so with the intention of one day being divorced. Each believes that this relationship will last until death, even if they've been married and divorced before. In spite of our initial preparation and commitment, here we stand. Once again, I say, there are no guarantees. There are choices that we make in the course of our lives that often determine where we end up.

We often look for a set of steps we can follow to achieve a desired outcome. We reason that if we do A, B, and C, the final result will be what we desire. Even if we get off track, we look for steps to get us back in line. The reality of this life is that there are often no easy formulas. Following the steps do not guarantee the results. My wife and I both read good Christian books on marriage, and sat under sound biblical teaching about marriage. We knew the right things to do, and even tried many of them. We also saw bad examples that we knew not to emulate. None of that kept us out of divorce court.

If anybody could endure the pain of a broken marriage, it was me. I was so used to pain. I was willing to stick it out as long as it took, while trying to make it better. It was rare for me to give up on anything. However, God was telling me that enough was enough. He had released me to be able to move on to what He had called me to do. Being released was not an easy concept for me to accept. I had doubts and questions. I asked God, "What about your Word that says, If I get divorced, can I get married again?" I didn't want to spend the rest of my life alone. I was still in my mid thirties.

After doing everything I could to salvage my marriage, I filed for divorce in the hopes that filing would bring my wife into accountability, and ultimately to repentance. I prayed that the process would not continue to completion. I had been adamant that I would not be the one to file for divorce. I was not going to be the one to break the vows. Divorce was not my choice. If my wife wanted a divorce, she would have to be the one to file. However, it became clear to me that I had to do something because my wife was not going to anytime soon. The marriage bond had already been broken by my wife when she chose to go outside the marriage sexually. She kept threatening to, but claimed she didn't have the money to file. It only cost $220 to file. She could spend that much on clothes on any given day. She had a good job, and her family and friends had been sending her money for other things. If the marriage was so bad, and I was the monster she portrayed me to be, they could have sent my wife the money to help her "escape from me".

My wife proposed that we stay together for the sake of the children. However, there would be no physical intimacy between us. She said she would not even talk to me unless it related to the children. She implied that I would be free to see other women, and she would do whatever she wanted to, though she denied she was having an affair. She was basically planning to use me for a roof over her head and convenience. I obviously was not going to go along with that plan. I had to protect our children. I could not continue to subject them to the drama they were experiencing on a daily basis. God was saying, "Trust Me. You don't see it now, but I have something better for you."

The first time I met with my attorney, I did not file the divorce paperwork. My attorney could sense that I was struggling with my decision to file. He advised me to come back when I was sure this was what I wanted to do.

The fact that I was the one to file for divorce also meant I couldn't be labeled as a victim. I wasn't sitting back letting things just happen to me anymore. I was being proactive. I took the power. That's what Jesus did with Judas when he was about to betray Him. He let Judas know He was aware of his intentions, and made him act on His terms. I'm convinced my decision caught my wife off guard. I believe she fully expected me to passively go along with what she was doing because she knew I desperately wanted the marriage to last. She was forced to make some decisions, rather than take advantage of my immobility. She was either going to decide to stay married to me or be with the other man.

Unfortunately, the more time passed, the worse the situation became. After the initial shock wore off, the act of me filing seemed to be a license for my wife to do whatever she wanted to. All bets were off. She told me she was actually glad I filed. "The fact that you filed," she told me, "lets me know that you realize it's over between us." "I don't have to worry about you pursuing me, trying to get back together." My wife did not understand my motive for beginning the divorce process. She saw it as incongruent on my part. She jumped at the opportunity to say that all the things I had recently said to her in an effort to save the marriage were all lies. How could I say I wanted to work things out, yet file for divorce? I believe in her mind, she could finally call me a liar and take the focus off her lies.

> *The notion of God releasing me from my marriage was a foreign concept to me.*

The notion of God releasing me from my marriage was a foreign concept to me. The teachings of my strict evangelical background did not allow for remarriage after divorce unless the spouse died. I understood that God hates divorce. At times I felt guilty for pursuing this course of action. I thought I was sinning by doing so. I expected a miraculous restoration to occur before the divorce process was completed. This had happened before when we were separated a few years earlier.

Our county requires that any divorcing parents with minor children attend a parenting class before the divorce is granted. The particular session I attended had about 30 parents. As I looked around the room and interacted with the people, I noticed that I was the only person wearing a wedding ring. There were a couple of women who had on engagement rings already, and they weren't divorced yet. I felt like an oddball. Surely I wasn't the only one in the group that didn't want a divorce. I was still married, and hoped that I would stay that way.

I hated the feeling I got every time I walked into that courthouse. It was like walking into a death chamber for families. It was full of attorneys who seemed to be only concerned about making money, or getting the most for their clients. Judges and magistrates appeared to be indifferent. Caseworkers seemed unconcerned about the human element. The faces of litigants expressed the pain in their hearts. It was like an assembly line.

> *The faces of litigants expressed the pain in their hearts. It was like an assembly line.*

When I was struggling with my decision to file for divorce, I sought the counsel of several godly people, including several pastors. I fully expected them to tell me that I needed to remain in my marriage and allow God to work the situation out. To my surprise, each one told me that divorce was my best and probably only recourse at that point. These individuals were familiar with the history of my marriage and had been personally involved with us at some level. They knew the hardness of my wife's heart, and were not getting just my side of the story. They were not surprised that I had come to this point, and seemed surprised that it had taken me so long to get there.

I knew I had biblical grounds for divorce because of the adultery, but that did not mean I had to choose that option. I needed the reassurance that I was not going against God's Word or His will. The Lord gave me a clear sense that He had released me from my marriage, and that this release was not in contradiction to His Word. He affirmed for me that I had been faithful to my vows and to my wife, and that I had done all that I could do. My wife had made it clear that reconciliation was not an option for her. The fact that there was a third party lover involved made the prospect of reconciliation nearly impossible. In the weeks and months that followed, God continued to show me that I was in His will, despite the guilt that Satan tried to dump on me. I experienced an overwhelming sense of peace.

There was a period of six months between the time I filed for divorce and my wife moved out of our house. That period was a living hell. Parts of that time frame are simply indescribable. There were times when I had to just get in my car and drive somewhere—anywhere—to get away from the madness. I thought things were bad beforehand, but nothing compared to this. I didn't realize the full impact until she was actually gone. When she left, there was an immediate sense of relief, and feeling that a heavy weight had been lifted from me. I no longer felt anxiety as I approached my house while driving home. Before then, I never knew what to expect when I got there. It was usually not good.

There were times when the police were called to the house for no reason. I figured she just wanted to have police reports on file to present at our divorce hearings. Sure enough, that's exactly what happened. The police reports clearly stated that there were no incidents. My wife indicated that she felt threatened, so the police advised her to leave. One of the officers said the following to his partner about me on the third incident:

"I've been to this house three times and I've never even heard him raise his voice." "I believe she's making these things up," he said about my wife. It bothered me that our children were witnessing this.

The first time, I was sitting in my car in the driveway talking on my cell phone when three squad cars pulled up in front of my house. My house is on a corner, with the driveway on the side, so I actually thought something was going on at my neighbor's house. The police officer was under the impression that I had driven to the house of my estranged wife to somehow harass her. I explained that I was still married, and I lived there.

Most of that time my wife treated me as if I didn't exist. We lived in the same house, but she refused to speak to me. It was worse than a roommate situation to me. I had a college roommate whom I didn't particularly like. He and I were at least cordial with each other. We had the common courtesy to acknowledge each other's presence. My wife would totally ignore me. I believe part of it was her extreme bitterness toward me, and part of it was the fact that she knew ignoring me would bother me. I did not appreciate her disrespect. I did not let it bother me for long, though. I understood her objective—to cause me to feel pain because of the pain I caused her.

My wife did not contribute to any of the household expenses. I was traditional in that way. I paid the mortgage, all utilities, insurances, etc. One hundred percent of the income she earned went to herself. She chose to pay for additional items for the children that she wanted them to have. I felt totally used. She was living in the house with me, consuming everything I was providing for her, yet she wouldn't open her mouth to even say "good morning" to me. Even when I would say good morning to her, she would just ignore me, or mumble something that was totally unintelligible. She would even do this in front of our children. They were watching her example. How could I teach them to speak when people speak to them, when mommy doesn't even speak to daddy when he says good morning. My wife would make it very obvious that she was ignoring me. When she would walk in the door after being away, she would say hello to our daughter and son by name, and not even look in my direction, though the three of us would be right together.

> *Later I realized that my actions were not holding her accountable, but were only enabling her to continue in her sinfulness.*

After a while I realized what she was trying to do, and did not let her actions bother me. I stopped wasting my breath speaking to her when I knew she wouldn't respond. Later I realized that my actions were not holding her accountable, but were only enabling her to continue in her sinfulness. I started doing what I knew I was supposed to do, and not letting her actions and responses dictate my behavior. She had to answer to God for her actions. Every time I spoke to her and she ignored me, she had to face what was in her heart.

Strangely enough, during much of this time, my wife and I were still sleeping in the same bed. There was obviously no intimacy, and there was no physical contact whatsoever. I had always heard of situations where a wife would get angry with her husband and make him sleep on the couch. I knew going in, that wouldn't be an option in my marriage. No matter what kind of disagreements we had, I was going to sleep in the bed.

Actually our bed was one of the few items my wife brought with her into the marriage. I thought she might try to use the "this-is-mine" strategy with me about the bed, but she never did. She did know my stance on that issue. It was only a full size bed, so she had to make an effort to not have at least incidental contact with me. She actually rolled up a spare blanket in a roll and put it between our "sides" of the bed, so our bodies wouldn't accidentally touch while we slept. She would also only sleep under the top layer of bed covering so we would not be under the same layer. If our bodies would happen to touch, there would be a sheet between us. I removed the barrier blanket.

For a long time I would intentionally stay on my side of the bed, and not touch her. Then again, I realized I was not holding her accountable. I would get in the bed and put my arm on her shoulder. She would get very angry and push my arm off, and tell me not to touch her. I would put my arm back on her shoulder, then she would get out of the bed and sleep on the couch. This scenario happened a couple of nights in a row, until she didn't bother getting in the bed anymore. She just slept on the couch or on the floor. From that day until the day she moved out, she never slept in the bed again. During the divorce proceedings she told her attorney I put her in a headlock and wouldn't let her get out of the bed.

The separate beds issue bothered me more for the sake of the children more than anything. They came to expect that parents don't sleep in the same room or bed together. Our bed became known as "daddy's bed". I wonder how this will impact their future marriages.

During this time, I was hired as the minister of music at another church. God orchestrated things such that I now had a one hour drive to church on Sundays and a couple of times during the week for various musical rehearsals. I would either be alone or have my children with me. They would often be asleep during the ride. I needed that time in the car to meditate and get my mind together from the things I just left at home, or what I was about to face when I got back.

At that point I was clinging to the hope that she would repent.

I considered hiring a private investigator to gather some physical evidence on my wife and her paramour. I had more than enough evidence of my own to know for sure that she was having an affair, but she continued to deny it. I wanted her to acknowledge her wrongdoing, but I did not want to tip my hand. I never told her what proof I had, so she thought I was bluffing or fishing for information. At first I naively believed that the court would be interested in the fact that adultery was occurring. I wanted to have something I could show her at some point. It was apparent to me that if there was ever going to be an acknowledgement from my wife, it would only be when faced with some undeniable evidence. At that point I was clinging to the hope that she would repent. I consulted my attorney, and he suggested that I would be wasting my money if I hired an investigator. He knew the court system, and that it wouldn't matter. My state has no-fault divorce laws. Since I didn't have the money to waste, I decided to forgo that option.

I actually spoke with a couple of investigators before I made my decision. After explaining my situation, one of them told me I had made his job easy. He often had cases in which the suspicious party didn't have much information to go on. I knew the man's name, address, license plate number, type of vehicle, and place of employment. He and my wife had a regular pattern that they followed on the weekends. The PI said all he had to do was follow my wife when she left the house and get the pictures I requested.

My wife took our children with her to her boyfriend's house on several occasions. My wife attended her boyfriend's family functions as if she was a part of his family. They actually treated her as though she were, from what I observed and heard in phone conversations. She bought his mother a mother's day card, and his daughter bought my wife a mother's day card. She blatantly displayed it on the shelf in our house. I'm not sure if she thought I didn't know who it was from, or if she was just being antagonistic.

She proudly displayed other gifts bought by him in our house—such as teddy bears. She claimed her godmother bought them, but I knew otherwise. She would talk to her lover on the telephone in my presence at times. Other times she would try to hide the conversations. Almost every morning my wife would get up and take her cell phone with her to the bathroom. We had a newly remodeled master bathroom, but she would go to the bathroom down the hall. She would turn on the shower and leave the water running for a very long period of time. This was to drown out the sound of her telephone conversations, so I could not hear them. She did not care about running up the utility bills, because she did not pay them.

Occasionally when she would talk to him on her cell phone, I could actually hear his side of the conversation, because the volume on her phone was up so loud. Sometimes it was obvious that she was baiting me. She wanted me to react out of my flesh so that she could have something else to use against me in the divorce proceedings. I didn't allow that to happen.

One Sunday while my children and I were at dinner after church, my 5-year old daughter mentioned my wife's boyfriend's name. I asked my daughter who that person was, to see what she would say. She replied, "That's Mommy's boyfriend." Needless to say I was outdone. I told my wife what my daughter said, and she accused me of lying on my daughter. "She didn't say that," my wife insisted. Liars tend to think that other people are lying, even when they aren't. They project their behavior onto others.

My wife was not very good at hiding what she was doing. She kept her mementos from her illicit relationship in her hope chest that was at the foot of our bed. I made copies of the cards and letters, and returned them to the chest. I also had phone records and photos I had taken of our car at her boyfriend's house and place of business on several occasions.

On the weekends, it was obvious when my wife was planning to go out with her boyfriend. She would spend considerable time in the bathroom getting ready to go "somewhere". When she came out, she would have on makeup, and be heavily perfumed. She was often wearing a new outfit that I had never seen before. She would then say she was going somewhere with one of her girlfriends. Her toothbrush would be missing from the bathroom, and a few times she left a bikini hair removal kit in the bathroom. She would then not return home until the following day, or the day after that.

I could always tell when she wasn't planning on coming home because her toothbrush would be missing. I couldn't understand how a person could go through such great lengths to hide an affair but wouldn't invest two dollars in an extra toothbrush. Every time the toothbrush was there, she would be home that night. When it was gone, it was at least an overnight trip. My kids would always ask me when mommy was coming back, and my answer would be based on the toothbrush. The overnight stays became so common that when my wife would leave, our daughter would say, "Mommy's not coming back until tomorrow."

She would sneak into the house through the back door, sometimes at two or three o'clock in the morning. We rarely used our back door. We almost always came in through the attached garage. The garage door opener was quite noisy, so it appeared this was her attempt to come in the house unnoticed. I would still almost always hear her when she came in.

After one of her trips, I found the duffle bag she had taken with her hidden in our closet. In it was some lingerie of hers that I had never seen before and two wine glasses from our wedding crystal. There was also soap and lotion from a hotel. She had told me she was going out with one of her girlfriends.

My wife's boyfriend's job often required him to be away during the week, so the weekends were their time to be together. On one occasion my wife came home with a hickey on her neck. I could not believe her audacity. Before she left, she said she was going out with her girlfriend. I'm sure that her girlfriend didn't put that hickey on her neck.

She had a calendar with her boyfriend's birthday and the anniversary of their relationship marked. Some of his family functions were also marked. She had requested time off from work to attend his family reunion.

After I noted her pattern, sometimes I would foil her plans. Just before she was about to leave the house, I would leave. She was then forced to try to find a babysitter at the last minute or cancel her plans. This made her even more angry with me, but I would not just stand by and watch her cheat. After a few times of me doing this, she planned ahead for someone to watch the children. Once she hired a babysitter to come to the house, but I was home as well. I guess she didn't want to take a chance on me spoiling her date. The babysitter was a college student from our church. I told the babysitter she could go home if she wanted to, but she said she didn't have anything else to do, so she would give me a break for that evening. I told her she probably thinks we're the craziest family she's ever met.

On one particular day my wife stopped at the grocery store on her way home from work. She picked up the ingredients for one her favorite recipes to prepare. It was a dish that required a lot of time and effort in the kitchen. This was notable because my wife had stopped cooking during this time period. She usually picked up some carryout food for herself and the kids. After she finished making this meal, she put some of it in a container. She told me she was taking some over to her girlfriend's house for her to taste it. Immediately I knew what was going on. She was taking this meal to her boyfriend. The thought of this disturbed me. She was using resources I provided to cook a meal for another man, and she wouldn't cook for me. Also, the container she used was not one of the plastic containers that one would normally use to put food in. It was one of our good glass dishes.

Right then, I knew what I would do. I was going to go to her boyfriend's job and see if she brought him this dinner. I left the house before she did, but I made a stop on the way. As I headed toward his place of employment, I saw my wife's car in my rearview mirror. I made a quick detour, and hoped she didn't see me. Sure enough, she was headed to his workplace. Her girlfriend lived in the opposite direction. I gave her enough time to get there, then I pulled into an adjacent parking lot. Her boyfriend's car was in front of the building, so I knew he was there.

I went inside and found my wife and kids in the front of the store talking to one of her female co-workers. Her boyfriend was not in sight. I could tell by the looks on both my wife's face and her co-worker's, that she was caught. I said, "I thought you were taking the food to your girlfriend's house. So you're making dinner for your boyfriend?" At that moment she became as angry as I had ever seen her in the entire time I'd known her. She began yelling loudly. I knew this was so that her boyfriend could hear her and stay hidden. She was so intense that she even frightened our daughter. My wife told me later that our daughter questioned why she was yelling at her dad. She told me this as she was scolding me for upsetting our daughter by showing up at this store. She accused me of following her. "I didn't follow you," I answered. "I left home before you did. You were going to your girlfriend's. I came here."

My wife claimed that her manager (aka, her boyfriend) was not in the store. I knew he was, because I saw his car. She didn't know that I knew his car and license plate number. He couldn't have walked home, because he lived almost 50 miles away. My daughter, who was shaken by this event, told me later that he was in the back of the store in the bathroom. He turned out to be a coward.

My wife changed her story to state that she brought dinner to this female co-worker, and not her girlfriend. I made my point and then left. Although I didn't get to catch my wife and her boyfriend physically together, my mission was highly successful. This incident came up later in divorce court as an example of me "stalking" my wife.

A few weeks after this, on a day when my wife returned home from one of her visits with her boyfriend, the dish appeared in the sink. I noticed her trying to conceal something as she came into the kitchen. I left the room and came back later after she went to another room, and found the dish underneath some other items in the sink. The fact that she put the dish under some other items indicated her guilt. Under normal circumstances, there would be no reason to hide the dish. She would just put it on top.

As I mentioned, my wife's boyfriend lived nearly 50 miles away from our home. When she would return home from her excursions, I would check the odometer on the car. Sure enough, there would be over 100 more miles on the car.

We had three vehicles at the time. One I had wrecked on Christmas day, after only having acquired it three days before. The car my wife was driving at the time was the car I normally drove. She had also recently had an accident with her car. It was still drivable, but not worth getting the damage repaired. She was embarrassed to drive it, so I switched cars with her. I didn't mind being seen in a banged up car. Also, I was the kind of husband who wanted his wife to be seen in the best light. If she looked good, I looked good.

This arrangement worked until the day I found evidence that my wife's boyfriend had been riding in our car. That was the last straw for me in relation to the car. Up until that time, I was only aware of her driving to meet him. I was not about to allow another man to ride around in (or drive) my car that I spent my hard-earned money to buy. From that day I took my car back from my wife. I didn't even tell her why. I just told her I was taking it back. I anticipated this would be a major battle, and it turned out to be just that.

My wife knew my concern for my reputation as a Christian husband and father, and tried to play that hand. It was difficult to resist her arguments, but I stood firm. She asked, "Are you going to let your children ride around town in a car that isn't safe? What if something happens to them?" I responded that they ride with me just as much, if not more. She told me that it was equally her car and mine because we were married. That was true, but only one of us could drive it at a time. It was interesting to me how she used the marital property argument when it was convenient for her. When she was emptying out our house when she moved, there seemed to be no marital property.

My wife was defiant and said she was going to continue to drive the car, despite my declaration. The next morning as she was leaving for work, I prepared for a showdown. As I expected, she got into the car and prepared to back out of the garage. As she pressed her garage door opener and the door began to go up, I pressed the opener inside the garage and closed it back. The door went partially up and down several times as our wills clashed. We argued as she sat in the car and I stood in the doorway. When I didn't give in, she threatened to call the police.

Again, she knew from the past that threatening to call the police was her ace in the hole. We both knew that at any time, she could accuse me of something, whether true or not, and call the police and have me arrested. They would likely believe her story because of the past. After all, she had been successful with this strategy in the past. The next time I would not be able to get off with just a plea. She knew I had a lot to lose.

I did not back down, however. "Go ahead and call the police," I responded. She took out her cell phone and made a call. I couldn't hear the conversation, but I stood there waiting for the police to come. I stood confidently, although on the inside I was nervous, realizing this could be a repeat of my first father's day. After several seconds, she got out of the car, got into the other car, opened that garage door, and drove off.

I don't believe my wife ever tried to drive that car again. She and her attorney went as far as to file a motion with the court to force me to give her sole use of that car. A hearing date was set, but as was typical in this process, the date was 6 to 8 weeks in the future. Before the hearing date came, my wife purchased another car. I don't know in whose name the car was registered, but it did not appear to be her name, because the county sticker on the plate was from a different county than ours. I don't know if she thought I would try to lay claim to any portion of it in the divorce, but I had no desire to.

At one point, I thought it would be good for me to just get away from all the craziness that was occurring around me. I decided to travel to visit my parents. I thought it would be a good trip for the children as well. They loved visiting their grandparents, and my parents loved spending time with them. I did not think it would be wise to tell my wife about my plans beforehand. We did not have a custody order at the time. As we were leaving, I called her from my car and told her that the kids and I were going to visit my parents for a week. I told her the specific day we would return. In the middle of the week, I got a call on my cell phone from my attorney. He informed me that my wife told the court that I had run off with our kids, and she had no idea where we were or when we would return.

She had also called the police and filed a report. In the back of my mind, I had a feeling this would happen, based on past experiences. That is why I gave her specifics on our trip. She made it seem like I kidnapped my children, like parents often do in custody disputes. She knew that was not the case. I had thoughts of seeing our faces on milk cartons or the weekly mailers for missing children. My attorney assured me that I had nothing to worry about, and I enjoyed the remainder of my vacation. The day we returned home, a local police officer showed up to see if we had made it home. The fact that he knew beforehand what day to show up, proved that my wife knew exactly when we were coming home. If my wife was unsure about the whereabouts of our children, she never called my cell phone even once to see where we were. I submit that the reason she didn't is because she knew where we were. Again, as scripted, during the divorce proceedings, my wife's attorney told the judge that I ran off with my kids.

I pray that no other couple will have to experience the pain that my wife and I have undergone. If someone had told me at the beginning of my marriage that I would be experiencing this particular set of circumstances, I would not have believed them. I could envision many possible scenarios, but not this one. Other couples I know who got divorced did not go through all the drama that we did. It still boggles my mind when I think about what has transpired and how it occurred. I had certain expectations when I entered marriage. Some were unrealistic, but many were not. I know, however, that none of this caught God by surprise. He was aware I would be right where I am, before the foundation of the world. He allowed it to happen, and has a plan for me that I cannot see right now.

This was a humbling experience for me. I did not think that pride was a big issue with me. I did begin to comprehend that my response to believers who had been divorced had sometimes been less than sympathetic. My desire to uphold the standards of truth from God's word sometimes caused me to be judgmental when it came to divorced couples. I often assumed they didn't want to work on their marriages. I didn't know their particular circumstances. Now I would soon be one of them. I would also have to face those who had witnessed the vows I made to God on my wedding day.

> *One must also know that God still has a plan and a purpose for his or her life.*

One must also know that God still has a plan and a purpose for his or her life. The fact that you are still alive assures you that God has something for you to accomplish. There is life after the failure.

The fact that my set of circumstances was so extreme, in my view, actually aided my recovery process. I understood that my situation was not normal. I couldn't view all of life from this perspective and fear the future. In my mind, the future had to be better than the past and present. There was no way it could be worse. I looked forward to what God had in store for me afterward. I praise God that He did not allow my heart to become bitter. My faith had not been shattered. I am not fearful of another relationship, if God would allow it. I believe I learned many things that would be helpful the next time around. I have a greater appreciation for the simple things and the important things in life. Things that used to concern me don't matter anymore. I am more free. I have less stress. I have gained weight. I enjoy life.

I am grateful for the opportunity to have experienced marriage, and the benefits that accompany it. For one, I wouldn't trade my daughter and son for anything. Only the union of my wife and myself could have produced the two unique individuals they are. Many people desire to get married, but never have that desire fulfilled. I would rather have experienced it and lost it, than not to have experienced it at all. I treasure many of the memories I have. There were points when I truly experienced love. I was also able to express love in a way that could only have been done in a marriage. I believe I have matured because of the experience, and have become a better person. I have a greater compassion for hurting people as a result of my own hurt. I'm not the man I was the day I walked down that aisle on that June afternoon.

> *I have a greater compassion for hurting people as a result of my own hurt.*

I'm also thankful for a second chance with my wife. If my wife and I had gotten a divorce the first time we were separated, I would probably now be living with a lot of "what-if" questions. I would be wondering what the outcome would have been if certain events had been different. The second chance gave me the peace of knowing I did all I could. I am not burdened by a lot of regret.

Support is another key to recovering from failure. I praise God for people He placed in my life to offer support and encouragement when I needed it most. Again I saw God's impeccable timing. A friend with whom I had lost contact over the years providentially showed up again in my life during this time. He had been through a divorce with similar circumstances, and was a great help to me. I saw how the Lord had worked in his life, and how he had become a better man through his experiences. Our personalities are also very similar, and he understood my perspective on many of the issues I was facing. Being able to talk and share with him was extremely helpful. Another close friend of mine was recently divorced, so the two of us could relate and support each other. Proverbs 27:17 states that iron sharpens iron, so one man sharpens another. These friends held me accountable. They did not just tell me what they thought I wanted to hear. I've had the experience of having people that I thought were my friends turn their backs on me when I was in a difficult situation. This caused me to value my friendships even more.

I also had tremendous prayer support. I had people all over the country praying for me, many of whom I did not even know. I would regularly get reports saying that people were keeping me in prayer. I had the support of my family, especially my parents. When I didn't have anyone else with whom I could share the details of the daily ordeals and drama, I could call them. They listened to me and encouraged me to hang in there. Sometimes just being able to talk about what was going on was therapeutic. I also journaled my experiences. That journal is the foundation for this book.

I had people who would tell me the truth, even when it was tough to hear. I was given some tough counsel, but I knew this person loved me and cared about my well-being. I trusted his wisdom. In the spiritual warfare I was facing, he counseled me to, number one, disengage out of strength, not passivity. This meant surrounding my wife with accountability, but not directly getting into a firefight. Secondly, he warned me not to trust anything she was saying to me. It was also suggested that I stop following her trails. He said the intelligence information was no longer necessary—I knew what was going on. The trails would just lead me to bitterness and sap my energy. He told me point blank—"It is over. It will not be pretty, but you battle to attempt to get her to see what her decision will cost." He advised me to accept the fact that I had been taken advantage of, manipulated, and lied to by my wife and others whom I trusted. He said I was fighting for God's righteousness at this point, not my vindication. That would come later.

Therefore, I was to fight with the strength and courage of a warrior—only offering tenderness in response to repentance. I was to offer the taste of defeat to open the door to repentance. He reminded me that my wife had moved on, and that I needed to do the same emotionally. The quicker the better. He also reminded me that my wife had always played my heart, and he cautioned me to not let it continue. I was given the following final words of advice: "Let go of hope. Her heart is too hard. Embrace the sadness of the loss and begin to reconstruct your life. There is much more life to be lived. Walk away from it. She is not big enough to destroy you. Save your heart's energy for your kids." Those were some powerful words of advice.

God wanted me to desire him more than I desired my wife. As a man, that is admittedly a difficult concept to embrace. Our image of God is as a male—our Father. Jesus is God's Son. He walked this earth as a man. When I think of the feelings and thoughts that I had toward my wife, it is difficult to correlate those same feelings and thoughts to a male figure. I've often heard women who have experienced relationship difficulty, or the lack of a desired relationship say that Jesus has become their lover. That is a whole lot harder for a man to say in our culture. In the Bible, our intimacy with God is compared to the intimacy between a husband and wife.

7

A View from Inside

Often times a change in setting offers a different vantage point on a scene. The same is true for viewing circumstances. A person's perspective changes when they go inside the house. Things look different inside the house. No one wants to be on the outside, looking in.

If Junior would go inside, he would no longer be in isolation. He might be able to learn something from his little brother's experiences.

The saying goes, "hindsight is 20/20". After you have experienced something, you are often able to see clearly things that you couldn't see while in the midst of the situation.

I have been able to look back and see God's hand in my life related to my current state. There were many situations that I didn't understand at the time, but I now see how the Lord used them to prepare me for where I am today.

The first company I worked for out of college was a subsidiary of a major corporation. After I had been there about four and a half years, the parent company decided to divest itself of our company. That left most of the employees, including myself, without a job. This was not a major hardship for me, though. I had never expected to work 30 years for any one company and retire, like many from the previous generation. I never intended for that particular occupation to be my lifelong career. I received a healthy severance package, and was financially set for a while. I didn't have a family or debt, so I knew I could make it for a while. I had a good education and now some work experience under my belt.

I began looking for a job, but was not desperate to find one. I shared with my church Sunday school class that I was job-hunting, and a few people offered me some leads. One particular person worked at a major corporation about 50 miles from where I lived. He gave me information about job openings and contacts where he worked. I graciously accepted the information, but really had no interest in working there. The main issue for me was the commute. It would take me an hour to get there in good weather. I had commuted to the job I had just left for quite a while, but it quickly became tiring, so I moved closer. I had no intention of relocating again for a job that could possibly be temporary. I was settled in my home and in my church. My extended family was about thirty minutes away.

This friend kept asking if I had done anything with the information he gave me, so I had to follow through to show my appreciation for his help. Shortly afterward, I was called for an interview. I figured I could always use the interview experience, but still had no desire to work at that company. I assumed this would be the standard short interview, and then

I could go about my day. It turned out to be one of those all-day affairs. I met with five different people, had lunch, took a tour, etc. I was frustrated because I really didn't want to be there. One of the interviewers was quite obnoxious, and because I didn't really care about getting the job, I wanted to respond negatively to him, but I restrained myself and acted professionally. It was a long, exhausting day. To my surprise, several weeks later, I received a job offer from that company

After starting there, it seemed that the Lord closed all the doors for any other position.

In the meantime I had other local interviews, and was awaiting offers from them. One in particular seemed very promising. I waited until the last day of the deadline I was given to accept the first job offer, hoping that another offer would come through. I reluctantly decided to accept this position. It was a very good job, but my time was very important to me. I did not want to spend a minimum of two hours per day just in a commute. I decided to take this job while continuing my job search. I had no intentions of staying there for long. I figured it was better to have this job than none at all. After starting there, it seemed that the Lord closed all the doors for any other position. I ended up working there for almost five years, until a door finally opened for me to work closer to home.

I gained a great deal from my experience at that company in a number of areas. I did not see it at the time, but God had me strategically placed there to prepare me for what He knew to be in my future. While at this company I developed some relationships with people and gained familiarity with the city where the office was located. I had no idea at the time that several years later my wife would be having an affair with a man who lived in that city, and would be taking our children there. It turns out that some of my friends there knew this man and his family. I was able to get valuable information that I probably never would have obtained otherwise. My familiarity with the city also helped me tremendously in other ways. I can look back and see some of the reasons God had me there besides the work experience. My wife eventually moved to this city.

A year prior to the divorce, I was under attack at my place of employment. I was being made the scapegoat for some financial loses that the company was taking. I had been in charge of some costly projects. One of my co-workers, who I believe was threatened by me, was actively trying to get me fired. My bosses were building a case to eventually terminate my employment. I was aware of what was going on, though they thought I didn't know. I continued to do my job to the best of my ability, even beyond the call of duty. The stress did take a toll, however. I discussed with my wife the idea of me taking a year off to concentrate on my own business, which I had on the side. My wife encouraged me to just quit the job right then, but I felt an obligation to complete the project I was working on. I willingly trained the person who was trying to get me fired. While he and I were on the jobsite, he would call back to the office and give a negative report about me to our management. When I felt the project was in a position to be turned over to my replacement, I submitted my resignation. This surprised my boss, especially when I told him I didn't have another job lined up. Essentially I was taking an early retirement at age 35! I felt good about leaving the job on my own terms and not theirs. Again, the Lord was preparing me.

As He allowed me to handle one attack, I gained confidence and skills for the next.

I've also seen God reveal truth (and Himself) to me in sometimes small, everyday things. He would often allow me to see things and/or discover information that I needed for a future time. At times I wasn't even looking for information, but facts were presented to me to confirm what was taking place around me. I would be at home at just the right time to hear a phone conversation or catch the mailman delivering a letter that refuted my wife's alibi on a particular day. These little incidents confirmed for me that God was watching, as He was Jacob when Laban was against him.

> *I began to see my faith work for me. I began to rest in the Lord and watch Him work.*

I saw God at work during the divorce process. There were some situations that could only be His doing. Even the attorneys who deal with these types of situations all the time, were surprised by one of the decisions made by the magistrate. I began to see my faith work for me. I began to rest in the Lord and watch Him work. There were many surprises. I looked forward to what was going to happen next. It was like reading a good mystery novel or watching a good suspense thriller. The outcomes were not always what I wanted, but I had confidence God was working out His plan.

As an example, both my wife and I petitioned the court to have the other party vacate our house during the divorce process. I knew the odds were heavily in her favor, based on the circumstances. The judge's decision was one that no one involved in the case anticipated. She ordered that neither one of us had to vacate, but that we had to continue to co-habitate. I was pleased with this decision, while my wife was outraged. I felt it was best for our children that our family remained under one roof for as long as possible. This arrangement would also make it more difficult for my wife to continue her affair. She would have some measure of accountability as long as we were in the same house. That ruling in itself was an indication that my wife was in no physical danger. If there had been any hint of a threat, I would have had to leave.

> *I took my stand for what I knew to be right and left the results with God.*

Ultimately, my wife decided to leave our house on her own and move to the city where her boyfriend lived. The court ruled that our children would live with her for school purposes. I have the children all but one weekend per month, and my wife and I split the summers and holidays with them.

I decided to take a chance and see if my wife's boyfriend would be willing to talk to me and fill in some of the missing pieces for me. I calculated that he would be my best hope for answers, though the chances were slim. I knew I would not get any information from my wife, and I had nothing to lose by asking him. I contacted him by email requesting a telephone conversation. His response to my email expressed his irritation at my contacting him, and he asked that I never contact him again. It may be best that I not know all the details.

The divorce process took two weeks shy of a year to complete. It was a long, tough experience. I believe I completed the assignment that God had for me. I was faithful to what He told me to do. Even though the final outcomes were heavily in my wife's favor, I have peace about the whole situation. It could have been worse. I took my stand for what I knew to be right and left the results with God.

> *Through this process, God confirmed for me that He was calling me into the preaching ministry.*

I discovered that taking a stand is viewed negatively by the court system. Compromise is their key objective in these proceedings. They encourage the parties to negotiate and come up with compromise solutions. I was dealing with some absolutes that couldn't be negotiated away or compromised. I was called uncooperative. I was accused by my wife and her attorney of being the reason the process took a year. They said I could have agreed to certain things much earlier in the process. They didn't understand my values. I had to let the process take its course. That was part of the consequences I had to force. I wanted the process to be over just as badly as my wife did, if not more. I was the one suffering. She had what she wanted. She didn't need divorce papers to maintain her affairs in the past, so what was the rush now? In my mind, the judge had to be the one to make certain decisions. Ten or twenty years from now, my children will not be able to say I negotiated certain aspects of their lives away. I can say with confidence that I fought the battle with all my heart and with integrity. I can hold my head up proudly.

Through this process, God confirmed for me that He was calling me into the preaching ministry. This was something I never anticipated, and honestly, didn't desire. From a child, people would tell me, "You're going to be a preacher one day." There were a number of preachers in my family, and I didn't want to be one. Once again, the Lord orchestrated events in my life to bring me to a place where He wanted me to be. I had to be open to God's direction in my life, even though this calling presented many questions for me. For one, was I qualified to be a preacher, having been divorced?

I can see how God has given me more compassion for hurting people. He had to prepare my heart for ministry. I still have a testimony of God's keeping power. It is no longer a testimony of keeping me "from", but one of keeping me "in spite of" and "in the midst of". I am still unsure of the direction the Lord is leading me, but I am trusting His plan for me.

> *I am still unsure of the direction the Lord is leading me, but I am trusting His plan for me.*

To my surprise, I have now been placed in a pastoral role under a senior pastor. My experiences have been invaluable in ministering to other people.

God had already given me a vision for a great task that has remained unfulfilled to this point. I asked myself the questions, "How did this calling fit into the task He had already given me to accomplish? How could I be effective as a divorced man?" I thought that maybe now that I am divorced, it was the opportunity to finally pursue the dream that had once burned in my heart. That remains to be seen.

God also made provisions for me financially. He worked out my job situation so that I had the flexibility to spend the maximum amount of time with my children. That was one of the reasons I quit my previous job. I was now earning a fraction of what I was accustomed to making, but God provided all of my needs. He also gave me favor in allowing me to advance in the company. I was in a totally different field, but I enjoyed what I did. In addition to that, I have been able to use my ministry gifts as a means of earning income as well.

God has also allowed me to meet and develop friendships with some godly women. This has reinforced for me that there is the potential for me to have what I still desire in a mate. These relationships have helped me confirm what I am really looking for, and what things I can accept and not accept.

I met a couple of women who had to choose between a relationship with me or another guy. In each case, I knew quickly that she was not the woman for me (or at least the timing was not right). If she has to make a choice, then the relationship is not going to work in my opinion. My belief is that there will always be questions in her mind about if she made the right choice, even if she chose me. I desire a woman who is fully convinced that Rodney is the man for her, and doesn't have to make a decision between me and somebody else.

To this point, our children have fared much better than I expected. It is still too early to know the full impact of all of this on them, but God has been gracious to my ex-wife and I in relation to the children. I believe they know that they are loved by both of us. We have not had behavioral problems with either of them, and they are both doing well in school.

I know the types of seeds I have planted throughout my life, so I am looking forward to my harvest. My curious nature still causes me to have many unanswered questions. But, if I don't get those answers, it's okay. I believe my vindication will come.

But in spite of that, I hear the music and the dancing. I smell the aroma of the feast. Things didn't turn out the way I expected, but I am choosing to go inside the house and experience God's presence and the celebration that accompanies Him. It's up to me. Rather than standing outside with my arms folded and brow furrowed, I am choosing to go into the house.

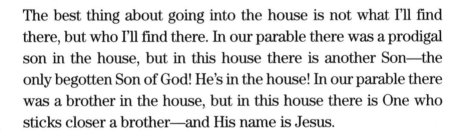

Rather than standing outside with my arms folded and brow furrowed, I am choosing to go into the house.

The best thing about going into the house is not what I'll find there, but who I'll find there. In our parable there was a prodigal son in the house, but in this house there is another Son—the only begotten Son of God! He's in the house! In our parable there was a brother in the house, but in this house there is One who sticks closer a brother—and His name is Jesus.

About the Author

Rodney A. Winters earned a BS in Electrical Engineering from Purdue University, and an MBA from the University of Akron. Along with his full-time job, he also serves as an adjunct professor of business at the Cleveland campus of Indiana Wesleyan University. Rodney is a staff minister at the Galilee City of Refuge Church in Akron, Ohio. He is gifted to preach and teach. He is also a musician, songwriter, and entrepreneur. He is the proud father of two children. Rodney's desire is to help people to embrace Christ's hope regardless of what they have been through in life. To find out more about Rodney Winters please go to www.rodneywinters.com

---

ALONE WITH A JIHADIST
A BIBLICAL RESPONSE TO HOLY WAR

By Aaron D. Taylor

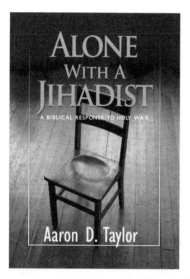

Alone With A Jihadist is not just another book about Islamic-Christian relations. It is far more than that. This book may very well be the solution to end many religious/quasi-political wars. While many fundamentalist/evangelicals tend to ascribe to a Zionist theology, which believes that it is good to be at war with anyone who opposes the Christian right, to expedite the glorious return of the Messiah, there is one crusader, Aaron Taylor, who believes otherwise. Taylor believes that the church has sadly missed the most pronounced message of Jesus Christ, the message of peace.

The very Bible, which Christians read, refers to their founder as The Prince of Peace. Despite this, many Christians support warmongering and unnecessary bloodshed rather than peacemaking. In a room for seven hours with a radical Muslim, Taylor shares the story from his face-to-face encounter, of how Islamic people view the United States of America, our present Administration, and the state of the Christian Church. It is one thing to look at Christianity from a Christians' perspective, which is typically an altruistic viewpoint, but things change quite a bit when Christianity is viewed through the eyes of Muslims. Taylor says, "Their [Muslims] view is one every Christian must hear!" This is the engaging story of that meeting.

ISBN 10: 1-934466-13-1
ISBN 13: 978-1-934466-13-1

Available Fall 2009
From Foghorn Publishers

The Obama Principle

Creating a Life of Reward through the Power of Perseverance

By Aaron D. Lewis, Ph.D

When you hear comments such as, "He's an overnight success" or "She just rose to stardom from out of nowhere" it makes you really ponder whether statements like those really have any value or if they are true. Do people suddenly appear out of thin air as overnight wonders? Or perhaps is it possible that while no one was watching, certain people were being tested, made, and crafted through though times and the bitter cup of rejection. The truth is; no one just makes it overnight. Whether you realized it or not, the great success stories of life all received their training on the "back side of the dessert" in the so called, "heat of the day."

Using the principle that President Barak Obama has reintroduced to the universe, you too can tackle the most unbelievable accomplishment and win at anything. In The Obama Principle, Aaron D. Lewis will show you how to conquer any dream, through understanding five simple supporting principles. Whether you are a business owner, educator, spiritual leader, politician, stay at home mother, peacemaker, humanitarian, or someone wanting more out of life, these time tested principles will ensure you guaranteed success. Use this winning formula, and embrace the reality that anything is possible.

ISBN 13: 978-1-934466-16-2
ISBN 10: 1-934466-16-6